WHAT IS THE NEW AGE SAYING TO THE CHURCH?

Also by the same author

Introducing the Old Testament
Introducing the New Testament
The Bible – Fact or Fantasy?
Tune in to the Bible

What is the

NEW AGE

saying to the

CHURCH?

JOHN DRANE

MarshallPickering

An Imprint of HarperCollins*Publishers*

Marshall Pickering is an Imprint of
HarperCollins*Religious*
Part of HarperCollins*Publishers*
77–85 Fulham Palace Road, London W6 8JB

First published in Great Britain
in 1991 by Marshall Pickering
3   5   7   9   10   8   6   4   2

A catalogue record for this book is
available from the British Library

ISBN 0 551 02286 8

Printed and bound in Great Britain by
HarperCollinsManufacturing Glasgow

For Tom and Jodi Pratt

CONTENTS

PREFACE

*I*T must be something like three or four years since I first
became interested in the New Age Movement. At the
time, I fondly imagined it would be possible to write a
book that would say something about the entire scope of
the Movement. Some of my initial reflections appeared in
my 1989 book, *The Bible: Fact or Fantasy?* There, I
attempted to say a little about New Age attitudes towards
the Bible and Christianity. The warm response that book
received has encouraged me to continue researching the
subject. In the meantime, the scope and influence of the
New Age Movement has continued to grow and spread at
an extraordinarily rapid rate. It includes a vast collection
of extremely diverse interests and concerns, and because
it is changing all the time it is very difficult to describe in
anything like a comprehensive way. What I have tried to
present here is a series of pictures of the New Age as I
have met it at particular times and places. Times and
places that were unique in themselves, but which seem to
me to be fairly typical of what is generally going on today.

In the process of gathering material, my main source of
information has been New Agers themselves. I have been
privileged to meet several of the world leaders of

the movement, as well as attending many New Age exhibitions, and investigating at first hand the New Age psychological and medical therapies. Naturally, I have also spent a lot of time reflecting on what it is all saying to me as a Christian. In the process, I have learned a lot – about the Christian gospel, as well as about the philosophies of the New Age. And about myself. I have not generally read many of the things that other Christians have written about the New Age Movement, and when I have, I have often been horrified by them, especially their vitriolic language and confrontational style – both of which seem to me to be seriously at odds with the way Jesus related to other people, even those with whom he had considerable disagreements. No doubt that explains why this is a very personal book, and presents its own distinctive Christian perspective on what is going on.

In reflecting on all this, I have been helped enormously by several opportunities to travel to far-flung places – Australia, south-east Asia, California – and meeting with people whose home is the two-thirds world has put the claims of the New Age Movement in global perspective for me, as well as enabling me to see western Christianity through the eyes of people for whom faith is not merely a hobby to be pursued in church on Sundays, but a matter of life and death every day of the week. If some of my criticisms of the western church seem a little too strident, and some of my opinions of New Agers a bit cynical, then my own exposure to the wider international scene is the reason for it. Westerners have always had the habit of taking themselves too seriously, and though we tell ourselves that imperialism is now a regrettable chapter in past history, the fact is that we have just exchanged political imperialism for a kind of intellectual and spiritual imperialism. If there is one thing that unites both western Christians and New Agers, it is the absolute conviction that they are right and everybody else is wrong. But things are rarely that simple, especially in the sphere of morality and religion.

Many people have helped in the writing of this book. Groups in universities, colleges, seminaries and churches across the world with whom I have shared workshops on the New Age Movement, and whose incisive thinking has at times challenged my own ideas, and occasionally led me to change them. Members of various New Age organizations, owners of New Age resource centres, and therapists of all kinds. And, as always, my special partner, Olive, and our children. Tom and Jodi Pratt looked after me in northern California during January 1990, and within the space of two weeks drove me something like 2500 kilometres as we visited one New Age centre after another. I liked their home and their company, and it gives me a particular pleasure to be able to dedicate this small book to them in gratitude for their help and their friendship.

John Drane
March 1991

Chapter 1

MAPPING OUT THE TERRITORY

*F*IVE years ago, hardly anyone had heard of it. I shall always remember having a meal with a leader of one of the mainline Scottish churches, and in the course of polite conversation he asked me what I was working on. No doubt he expected me to name some book of the Bible, or some abstruse theological topic. But he could hardly conceal either his surprise or his curiosity when I replied, 'The New Age Movement'. For one thing, he had no idea what it was. And when I began to describe it to him, he could hardly believe what he was hearing. He was too polite to say it, but it was perfectly obvious that he went away wondering how and why I could possibly be wasting time investigating something this crazy. Now all that has changed. The very same church leader recently set up a major conference on the New Age Movement for his denomination, and invited me to be the keynote speaker!

Things have obviously moved very fast, and there can be few westerners today who have not met the New Age Movement somewhere. New Age thinking and terminology has permeated into every significant area of life. Its concepts are taken for granted as the raw materials out of which the plots for Hollywood movies are structured. It is one of the most frequently discussed subjects on TV chat shows. It has generated a whole new style of music. There are New Age books by the thousand – and even the smallest bookstores boast a New Age section. No one could deny that the New Age has taken the entertainment scene and the media by storm.

But you are as likely to find it in more reflective and serious places too. New Age devotees include lawyers and sober-suited business people doing self-improvement courses and using overtly spiritual techniques for handling corporate stress management, wealth creation and relationship and communication training. New Age thinking has given birth to new disciplines, such as transpersonal psychology. And many educational institutes take New Age concepts as the basic starting points for their courses. In England, the old Lancashire mill town of Skelmersdale is the unlikely home for the Maharishi School of the Age of Enlightenment. Here children aged from three to sixteen study using the Unified Field Education System, which is based on a theoretical concept called the Science of Creative Intelligence. New Age therapies and spiritual techniques form part of the everyday curriculum and help create an atmosphere which headmaster Derek Cassells believes makes the children more relaxed in relating to the staff and more willing to learn. If they go on to higher education, children of schools like this could well find that the California Institute of Integral Studies would be the right place for them. Its catalogue of degree programmes lists courses on all kinds of esoteric religious topics, including Shamanic Art and Ritual Healing, Nutrition and Spiritual Growth, the Re-emergence of the Goddess, Voice, Psyche and Spirit, and Learning to

Heal. And even mainstream, 'secular' educators world-wide are having to face up to claims that the performance of schoolchildren can be improved by techniques such as breathing and relaxation exercises, fantasy games, yoga, transcendental meditation and making contact with 'spirit guides'. Alongside all this, fitness freaks have developed a bewildering array of unconventional health cures and psychological therapies.

Suddenly, it's trendy to be spiritual. In her book *Stare Back and Smile*, British actress Joanna Lumley puts it succinctly: 'More spirituality and less materialism are what we need in the West . . . In the 1990s we're going to start finding our souls again. We've gone through a very non-spiritual time this century.'[1] After the hippy scene of the sixties, the rock and drugs of the seventies and the radical materialism of the eighties, it is now time for a more spiritual way of life that will see us safely through the nineties, and on into a new century and the next millenium. There have always been people who have thought that way. But what was once regarded as a minority interest – the preserve of idealists who patronized wholefood shops, burned joss-sticks and read the works of eastern mystics – has now become big business. It is fashionable to be Green and spiritual.

SEARCHING FOR DEFINITIONS

But what exactly is the New Age Movement? That was the question I put to a black basketball coach over breakfast one day at a homely coffee shop in Piedmont, California. After a long period of reflexion, my companion – known to me only as TJ – put it like this: 'Think of the New Age Movement as a vacuum cleaner,' he said. 'It picks up whatever is there, and messes it all up. So when you open the bag, you recognize all the bits and pieces that are in there – but the mixture is completely different from anything you've ever seen before, or anything you could even imagine. You probably wonder how it can all possibly belong together. The fact is, it doesn't. Those things are in there just because the vacuum cleaner happened to pick them up. If it had moved in a different direction, it would have sucked all kinds of other things in. They would look quite unlike the first collection – but they would be "New Age" as well.'

Back in Europe, I posed a similar question to a friend who makes his home on a remote island off the west coast of Scotland, and is about as far removed from a typical Californian as you could imagine. After a moment's thought, he described the New Age to me as 'the sweepings of the ages'. At least the two of them agree!

But these are not simply the emotive reactions of people with a casual acquaintance with the subject. Stephen Dunning, a professor of Religious Studies at the University of Pennsylvania, compares the New Age to catalogue shopping – it is a kind of supermarket of spiritual and emotional goodies, from which customers may choose whatever they think will meet their needs. While Robert Ellwood, another Religion professor at the University of Southern California, is quite convinced that, whatever it is, the New Age is definitely not new. 'It is characterized,' he claims, 'by the recovery of a lot of very old things in spirituality that have been lost over the years, partly due to being eclipsed by the so-called great religions.'[2] For decades, if not centuries, we have been told that the world is not a sacred or mystical place, and that it can be explained quite simply by the discoveries of modern science and by an understanding of the laws of nature. Nowadays people are not so sure, and increasing

numbers are searching for spiritual explanations of what
is going on.

At the same time, the New Age is definitely not a
religion. It is not even a belief system in the traditional
sense, and it is certainly not a cult. There is nothing to
join. Nor does the Movement have a headquarters. New
Age people might be doing literally anything, and a
quick glance through any New Age directory reveals a
bewildering variety of options all wearing this label. In
The Blue Pages – a New Age equivalent of the Yellow
Pages, published by Prasada Hamilton in Western
Australia – colour analysts rub shoulders with transpersonal psychologists and New Age musicians, while
university courses in consciousness studies compete for
customers with eastern gurus and Gnostic priests. All
of these options offer personal transformation and
self-discovery through therapies that range from traditional homoeopathic medicine through to healing with
crystals, past-life recall and advice from entities in outer
space or some other spirit world. Alongside this concern
for personal development is a deep-seated anxiety about
the future of our polluted planet – a commitment that
may be expressed through actions ranging from regular
membership of an environmental pressure group to
life-changing pilgrimages to remote deserts and
mountainsides, spiritual communication with dolphins
and whales and involvement with any one of a multitude
of rituals designed to enhance attunement to Gaia,
the earth goddess. As the preface to the Californian
New Age directory *Common Ground* puts it: 'there
are undoubtedly as many paths to personal transformation as there are people . . . Whether a resource
is useful to your personal transformation is a matter
of attunement: it's a matter of resonance between

what the resource is and who you are at this moment in time.'

Not surprisingly, it is quite challenging to try and define the New Age Movement, not least because some New Agers are now backing off from using the term 'New Age' at all. Kenny Kaufman, producer of San Francisco's annual Whole Life Expo, is one of them. 'It was OK in the '70s to say "New Age",' he explained, 'but now people think "rip-off" when they see "New Age". So we're now calling it the new era of awareness.'[3] Hemitra Crecraft and Sue King, who caused a stir among the conservative inhabitants of Pennsylvania when they first opened their Chester County New Age emporium, also admit, 'We don't even call ourselves New Age' – adding, 'it has the connotation of the occult.'[4] A sentiment with which Hollywood superstar and New Age evangelist Shirley Maclaine would agree: 'Millions of people all over the world are so interested in this stuff,' she writes, 'that they support an entire industry of books, teachings, schools, individuals, and literature of all kinds devoted to the metaphysical dimensions of life. I wouldn't call it the occult anyway. I would call it an interest in the spiritual dimension of life.'[5] On the other side of the Atlantic, Carol Riddell of Scotland's Findhorn Community agrees: 'We are now a little wary of this [New Age] description, which was once eagerly embraced by the Findhorn Community, because in popular thought it has become connected with the sensation seekers . . . whose interest lies less in seeking spiritual transformation than in dabbling in the occult, or in practising classical capitalist entrepreneurship on the naive.'[6]

Whatever you call it, it's no easier to comprehend. The amazing diversity of the ingredients that go into the New Age mixture will always ensure that any definition we come up with can, with perfectly good reason, be

challenged by someone else whose experience of it has
been quite different. It's like a movie with a constantly
changing plot, being produced by a director who writes
the script only after he does the filming. Nobody knows
which way things will move next – and it probably doesn't
matter. The most helpful way to begin to understand it all
is therefore to focus on just a few examples of what the
New Age Movement might look like at particular times
and places. A series of stills from the larger movie, if you
like. Or bits from the vacuum cleaner, if you prefer the
other image. They won't tell the whole story, but they will
highlight some of the central ingredients.

There are obvious weaknesses in starting this way. For
one thing, it means that I can only present the New Age
Movement as I have met and experienced it for myself.
This is an authentic view, but certainly not a complete
one. If I had been in different places and with different
people, I would certainly have seen different things.
There will always be a danger of missing something really
significant. On the other hand, to begin with a simplified
picture can also help to pin down what is otherwise a very
diffuse collection of theories and ideas. So with these
qualifications in mind, let's begin to map out the territory
by taking a brief look at four stills from this unfinished
movie that is the New Age Movement.

MIND AND BODY

Our first stop – inevitably – has to be Hollywood. Where
else, you might ask, would you go to find an insight into
something as trendy and glamorous as the New Age
Movement? Here, actress Shirley Maclaine has emerged
as probably the best known representative of the
whole phenomenon. Through her TV interviews and

newspaper and magazine articles – and especially through the autobiographical book *Out on a Limb*, which formed the basis of the TV mini-series of the same name – she has done more than anyone else to alert ordinary people to the fact that some remarkable things can happen when people become seriously involved in a search for spiritual meaning in life.

Her own story is typical of many American people. Since they were brought up in a traditional Baptist home, God was a natural part of life for both her and her younger brother, actor Warren Beatty. For this family, going to church was as normal a part of everyday life as going to school or the supermarket. As a child and a teenager, Shirley Maclaine simply took religion for granted and committed herself to what she knew and understood of the teachings of Christianity. But as adolescence gave way to adulthood, with all the demands of a home and a career, she gradually let go of her involvement with Christianity, and in due course drifted away from the church altogether. Not because she ever took any conscious decision to reject it: it was simply no longer as relevant as it had once seemed, and therefore its importance naturally declined.

So what's new? This must be the personal story of vast multitudes of people brought up in traditional western Christianity. And what followed is no less typical. For when Shirley Maclaine drifted away from the church, she did not lose her faith in religion in the broadest sense – nor was it possible for her to suppress her deep conviction that if life has any real meaning, the key to it all must be found in the realm of the spiritual and the supernatural. Personal maturity and professional success created within her a deeper fascination for and growing commitment to the search for some spiritual meaning behind it all. Like many of her generation, she began to wonder if other cultures – especially mystical eastern religions – might have more to say than her own strict Baptist background. Unlike most of her contemporaries, she was rich enough to be able to fly around the world with ease, consulting spiritual guides on several continents, and frequently following in the footsteps of pop stars and actors to India, Nepal, Tibet and similar esoteric destinations. All of which was interesting, and occasionally helpful. But she only began to find something that spoke to her when she became personally aware of the existence of a whole spiritual realm that is beyond and above the things we can see and touch and handle in everyday life. As a result of a chance meeting with people who claimed to be receiving messages from spiritual entities in some other world, she found herself inescapably drawn into a systematic and determined effort to get to the bottom of it all. Her quest eventually took her to the top of the Andes mountains in Peru, where she had a remarkable experience.

To cut a long story short, she was persuaded that by immersing herself in warm mineral springs flowing at the top of the Andes, she could find the pathway to a renewed spiritual awareness. It sounded unlikely – and she herself was sceptical. But as she put it to the test, the most amazing things began to happen. As a result of the combination of the water, the aroma and various breathing exercises, she found herself disengaging from her body and rising into some higher form of existence. In her own words,

My head felt light. I physically felt a kind of tunnel open in my mind . . . I had no arms, no legs, no body, no physical form. I became the space in my mind. I felt myself flow into the space, fill it, and float off, rising

out of my body until I began to soar. I was aware that
my body remained in the water. I looked down and saw
it . . . My spirit or mind or soul, or whatever it was,
climbed higher into space. Right through the ceiling of
the pool house and upward over the twilight river . . .
wafting higher and higher until I could see the
mountains and the landscape below me . . . attached to
my spirit was a thin, thin silver cord that remained
stretched though attached to my body in the pool of
water. I wasn't in a dream. No, I was conscious of
everything . . . it felt like a new dimension of
perception, somehow, that had nothing to do with
hearing or seeing or smelling or tasting or touching . . .[7]

The silver cord which she saw ensured that in due course
she did return to her body. This first experience of what
she later came to recognize as astral projection left a deep
and lasting impression on her. It provided the opportunity to be in touch not only with her own inner self but
also with another strange world of expanded consciousness, in a way that would ultimately give a radically new
meaning and direction to her entire life.

Many people have reacted to all this with cynicism and
disbelief. They have argued that anyone could induce
the same experiences by engaging in regulated breathing
exercises while immersed in warm water in an oxygen-
starved atmosphere – and that far from putting a person
in touch with some new spiritual world out there, it is
nothing more than psychological manipulation. In his
review of the five-hour-long TV movie of this story, John
Carman, television critic of the *San Francisco Chronicle*,
described it as 'deliriously wacko', and went on to wonder
whether Shirley Maclaine was, as he put it, 'out on a limb
or just plain off her rocker'.[8]

There is no doubt that New Agers need to address themselves to comments of this sort with more rigour than they do, and to back up personal experience with something that can be tested by other people. But it would be pointless to deny the profound impact that such experiences are having on the lives of many ordinary people. Shirley Maclaine's story has been broadcast around the world only because she happens to be famous. But there are tens of thousands of people whose stories parallel hers – and not a few who claim even more spectacular experiences as they pass from one dimension of consciousness to another. Not many can afford either the time or the money to travel to distant lands, but local therapy centres have sprung up all over the western world, offering similar spiritual adventures at a modest price. Here 'rebirthing' (as it is often called) takes place in the more domestic atmosphere of a hot tub or jacuzzi. Attended by a therapist with experience of such things, and with a water temperature of fifty degrees centigrade and twenty minutes or so of controlled breathing, anyone can readily enter a trance-like state leading to a suspension of sensation in the arms and legs, as the spiritual pilgrim floats in a watery universe that, it is claimed, will ultimately give new meaning and direction to life. Three sessions is reckoned to be the minimum requirement to produce some lasting change, but many people 'rebirth' like this once a week. Not always in a hot tub, for the experience can also be carried out 'dry' – and at lower cost – on a futon mattress. But the watery context is generally preferred. It is certainly more intimate, and is also claimed to accelerate the process of change, leading rapidly from one dimension of consciousness to another in an almost infinite variety of personal spiritual adventures.

IS THERE ANYONE OUT THERE?

Not all New Agers go in for rebirthing, or anything like it. Some go to the theatre – or, more often, a hotel – to get in tune with themselves and the larger cosmos, in a process called channeling. To see what this was all about, I joined a crowd of several hundred people jammed into a large auditorium in North America. As we lined up outside the theatre waiting to pay $15 each to get in, the atmosphere was electric. There was an almost tangible mood of buoyant expectancy as people handed over their cash and headed for the door. Even the casual visitor could not fail to appreciate that something special was about to happen. And indeed it was. For the featured star of this performance was not Shirley Maclaine – nor any other human actor. It was a 35,000-year-old warrior from the lost city of Atlantis, who goes by the name of Ramtha. This just had to be the show to end all shows, and as the audience settled into their seats for the evening, you could tell that they knew it.

As things got underway, one or two looked anxiously about them, wondering if, after all, they had been conned. For the person who appeared on stage was the exact opposite of a macho barbarian warrior: an unassuming female homemaker from Oregon, by the name of J. Z. Knight. However, the audience was soon reassured, as her voice took on a lower pitch and even her physical appearance underwent a subtle change – and it was obvious that she was not alone. By now, 'Jayzee' was no longer an ordinary American woman: she had become a channel for a message beamed in from some other world – the world of extraterrestrials and spirit guides. A world inhabited by beings – 'entities', as they are often called – of far greater wisdom than ordinary mortals, who can see things in a much wider perspective than we can, and who, it is claimed, have a special role at this point in history, to alert the human race to the real meaning of life.

As 'the Ram' delivers his message, the audience listens intently to every word. He may well be a very old soul, but when it comes to the fears and concerns of western people living at the end of the twentieth century, he certainly seems to know what he's talking about. The crisis in the environment, justice and peace, world politics, feminism, personal spirituality – Ramtha has an angle on all these, and more. His speech at times sounds a bit archaic, as befits a message from someone who lived in the distant past, but it all comes over with great clarity and considerable persuasion. As the monologue comes to an end and Ramtha makes himself available for further discussion, many eager hands are raised by those who want to ask him questions. Someone wonders which is the most suitable supermarket for people of developed consciousness to buy their groceries at. Another enquirer asks about the prospects for world peace, and whether a messiah figure will be needed to make all the nations toe the line. An anxious young woman confides that she would like to have a baby, and asks for advice about the most auspicious time to conceive – an enquiry that, surprisingly, receives as specific an answer as the question about the supermarket, with precise details not only of the month, but also the day of the month, and even the time of day. In the face of such prodigious knowledge, there is naturally no shortage of questions. But eventually even extra-terrestrials have to withdraw, and the event draws to a conclusion – though not before Ramtha has made it clear that he can be consulted by personal appointment at other times and places. The charge for this? Something like $400 for a typical session – payable by credit card, of course. Ramtha may be an ancient spirit, but he has connexions in all the right places in the modern world. As Ramtha returns to his celestial dwelling, the punters go out into the cold night air fired with a new enthusiasm to share the New Age message of spiritual awareness with those outside who are still living in an unconscious darkness.

People whose only spiritual diet has been traditional western Christianity find all this somewhat far-fetched and unbelievable. But when Ramtha speaks, people sit up and take notice. Many, including several well-known Hollywood stars, have moved home in order to be closer to J. Z. Knight and have his celestial wisdom more easily accessible. During a 1988 tour of Australia, when Ramtha delivered a warning in the ballroom of the Hyatt-Kingsgate Hotel in Sydney that a tidal wave 'higher than your highest building' would flood over the city, many of the audience went straight out to sell their homes and move to higher ground.

But this is just one example. Unlikely as it might seem, the fact is that thousands of people all over the world are in daily contact with such spirit guides. Their advice is sought not only at times of crisis, but on a regular basis as a source of empowerment for daily living. It has even been alleged that people in positions of public responsibility and influence have consulted such entities when faced with potentially world-changing decisions. In 1988, former White House chief of staff Donald T. Regan claimed that US President Ronald Reagan and his wife used an astrologer to plan their lives. According to a report from Associated Press dated 3 May 1988, it was on such advice that he insisted on signing a nuclear disarmament treaty with the Soviet leader Mikhail Gorbachev at exactly 1.33 p.m. on 8 December 1987. At the time, Reagan denied making policy decisions on such a basis, but his wife's press secretary subsequently confirmed that Nancy regularly consulted 'a friend that does astrology'. There have been many examples of schoolteachers utilizing similar techniques in the classroom, introducing children to their 'friends' from other worlds who can give guidance and counsel when more ordinary relationships, with parents and family, break down.

Channeling has become big business, and Ramtha is just one of thousands of spiritual 'entities' whose advice and wisdom is valued as a trustworthy guide to the precarious business of living in the modern world. Relationships, goal setting, health and career advice – there are spirit guides to advise on all these matters, and more besides. And they can as easily be consulted over the phone as by personal attendance at a large channeling session. In the words of Kay Brockway, a Californian channeler of 'Michael' ('an entity of 1,050 souls who have finished their work in physical bodies and now reside on the Causal Plane'), such extraterrestrial messages bring 'a unique philosophy of understanding our personal essence and personality . . . of great assistance in supporting your truth by helping you move through obstructions to higher self-esteem and prosperity'.

CRYSTALS

Spirit guides are only one way of tapping into the celestial energy that, it is claimed, will bring healing and wholeness into life. Sometimes very obviously tangible and physical objects can be used for the same purpose, most notably crystals. They are big business, and stones that twenty years ago no-one would have bothered with are on display in the crystal stores that have multiplied in towns and cities all over the western world. Here stones of all sizes, shapes, colours and textures may be tried out and, of course, purchased. A 1990 issue of *TS Beat*, the youth magazine of a major UK bank (subsequently withdrawn after customer complaints), claimed that 'crystals contain certain life-enhancing, healing properties', went on to recommend that 'clear quartz is the best', and then advised its readers that 'a crystal around your neck is fashionable as well as saying you're a sensitive energised individual'.[9] The promotions for many collections of designer clothes and jewellery have used crystals. It is even possible to buy what the founder of the Bodylove company calls 'metaphysical underwear' – the New Age answer to erotic lingerie. Except that here, open crotches are replaced by specially constructed pockets to allow wearers to place their favourite healing crystals next to their body's energy centres, thereby ensuring continued wholeness and vitality throughout the working day! And in case that doesn't work you can have your metaphysical belt-and-braces by wearing a pair of 'Chi-pants' on top – fashionable outer garments that work on the same principle.

Crystals can cost as little or as much as you are prepared to pay. But choosing a crystal requires considerable discernment. Not just any crystal will do. In the words of Debbie Hogerdyk, who runs a crystal store in Western Australia: 'Every crystal is individual. It interacts with your personal energies, so you have to feel what's right for you.' Crystals are supposed to vibrate at a particular level, and if you come across one you like, that means it is vibrating at the same level as you. Discovering the right one can be a simple matter of holding a stone in your open hands, or it may require a complex procedure involving meditation, chanting and other overtly mystical techniques. And like many other things in the New Age market-place, it can often be expensive. I remember overhearing a conversation at a New Age exhibition. A woman was trying to decide which crystal to buy. She had her eyes on a small stone, the price of which was a mere four US dollars. But the salesperson was determined that she should have the best possible advice in making her decision, and insisted on placing several different stones in her hand, so that she might feel what was best for her. Almost inevitably, the one that felt most right turned out to be much more expensive, priced at just over $400! It obviously had good vibrations for the salesperson.

So what will crystals do for you? That was a question I put to the owner of a crystal store in Berkeley, California. Crystals are not only good for business, she explained – they are also a focus of considerable power. Especially quartz fingers, which were carefully packaged in a box with a slightly threatening sign: 'These crystals have supercharged energy: please do not point them at other people.' Naturally, I avoided them, and went instead for other, safer stones beginning with hematite which the assistant assured me would 'ground' me – Aquarian-speak for putting me in tune with my own inner self, but also ensuring that I would not be caught up in levitation or other astral wanderings before I was ready for it. Then, having been glued to the floor, personally and meta-physically speaking, it would be safe for me to try out some of the other stones. In this case, the trial was a simple matter of visualization. You had to close your eyes, hold the crystal in your hand, do some heavy breathing and put your imagination to work. You would form a mental picture of the crystal as a source of great light and energy, which would gradually creep into your hand, up your arm, and into the centre of your being, where it would clean out all negative feelings and forces – its healing powers gradually displacing them and, hopefully, leaving the subject with a sense of greater wholeness, well-being and 'balance'. In a sense, the presence of the crystal is not strictly relevant for this kind of exercise, for it merely serves as a focus for the natural processes of the imagination.

Most crystal devotees would go much further, and regard the crystal itself as the embodiment of some kind of spiritual power. The reasoning behind this highlights the intriguing relationship that exists between New Age thinking and the modern scientific community. Crystals – silicon – are at the heart of the modern computer industry. They are remarkably efficient conductors of electrical energy. Hence the belief that they are good conductors of other kinds of energy too – like psychic energy, spiritual energy, and even the essential energy fields of the whole cosmos. In a chemical sense, of course, crystals can be thought of as the essence of the cosmos: the distillation in its purest form of the elements that go to make up the natural world. To be in contact with crystals is therefore to connect with some primal life forces of the earth.

New Agers generally believe there is an energy field running through and permeating everything, from rocks to people. In this frame of reference crystals are a way of getting your own personal energy in tune with such cosmic energy. In the words of Korra Deaver, 'Crystals act as transformers and harmonizers of energy. Illness in the physical body is a reflection of disruption or disharmony of energies in the etheric body, and healing takes place when harmony is restored to the subtler bodies. The crystal acts as a focus of healing energy and healing intent, and thereby produces the appropriate energy.'[10] This cosmic energy is perfect and all-embracing and so by tapping into it through crystals one can strengthen any weak areas in the human body and correct any negative influences in it. In the first *Superman* movie, the baby who later becomes Superman hurtles towards the earth in a capsule made of crystals – crystals in which the total intelligence of all the galaxies is said to be contained. Through them he has access to all that wisdom. But you can also learn how to programme a crystal with your own thoughts. Many practitioners claim that particular crystals can cure quite specific ailments, both physical and personal. Simon Thomas, manager of London's Aurora Crystals, explains it this way: 'There is a yearning inside us now for balance, for finding out why are we here. The energy inside a crystal is always looking for balance. You could talk about disease as being a state of imbalance. Crystals redress this. They have the capacity to bring out what is lost and forgotten.' There is a whole hierarchy of crystals, each of them with its own specific healing properties. So, for example, amethyst will aid self-confidence, as well as healing anaemia, insomnia, headaches and colds, while rose quartz can encourage creative thinking, and citrine will help to control the emotions and promote a sunny disposition.

Not all New Agers use crystals. But the claims made for them are only a small part of a wide-ranging belief in alternative healing therapies of all kinds, in which traditional homoeopathy and faith healing rub shoulders with more overtly New Age treatments, mostly deriving from oriental mysticism. This has been one of the great New Age growth centres of recent years. It is eagerly embraced by pseudo-religious groups and is also being increasingly welcomed within orthodox western medicine.

IMPROVING PERSONAL PERFORMANCE

For the final part of our introductory tour of the New Age Movement, we pay a visit to the corporate world of big business. Many people would have nothing to do with the Movement if they first encountered it as a religious or spiritual phenomenon. They would automatically relegate it to the irrelevant fringe, along with Moonies, Mormons, Jehovah's Witnesses – and, for many, the mainstream Christian churches. But it all sounds much more serious and convincing when they meet it in the course of training for their everyday work. So how does New Age thinking operate in an environment that appears to have little room for spirituality?

It is difficult to generalize, for management training consultants are not always happy for their courses to be labelled 'New Age'. But here is one example of something that actually happened in a multi-national corporation in Scotland and which, give or take the odd detail, is fairly typical of what is taking place in many parts of the world.

A group of top executives had been told they were to go on a management course to improve their skills. Their preliminary instructions were very basic, and all they knew was that they were to present themselves at their workplace early one morning, with a suitcase packed for a course that would last most of the week. They had no idea where they were going, but that hardly seemed important, since it is normal business practice for even trivialities to be kept under wraps until the last possible moment. They set off from the company's headquarters in their usual grand style: a fleet of immaculate limousines which would take them the short distance to the nearest airport. There they boarded an unmarked executive jet for a destination still unknown. There was nothing especially unusual about that either, for most company aircraft carry no markings in order to preserve the shroud of commercial secrecy that is believed to be essential for the successful running of a big business. In any case, they took this as a sign that they could expect to enjoy themselves, maybe in an exotic location. During the flight much food and drink was consumed, and the passage of time was hardly noticed. As one participant told me, they were all enjoying themselves so much that it felt like thirty minutes, though they had actually been travelling for nearer three hours by the time they touched down at a private airstrip.

There were no signs to tell them where they were, and some of them were surprised to find no customs or immigration formalities waiting for them. But they had all been on courses like this before, and knew there was nothing to worry about. In any case, they were obviously not at their final destination, as their jet had come to a stop alongside a fleet of helicopters, which were waiting to take them to journey's end. Two-by-two they were assigned to different helicopters and unceremoniously whisked away. This time, their luggage was left behind – and after a short while the terrain beneath began to look decidedly rugged and inhospitable. They also noticed that the helicopters had not all gone in the same direction, and some began to wonder what had happened to their colleagues. However, such speculation was cut short when the chopper carrying the two we are following began to make its descent. As they peered out through the mist that now surrounded them, they began to sense that things were not quite what they seemed. They were not, after all, at a conference centre. In fact, they were not anywhere recognizable at all. They were just beginning to wonder if they had been kidnapped when the crew of the helicopter bundled them out into the cool air of early evening. They found themselves standing on the soft turf of what turned out to be a very damp moor. They were handed a piece of paper with just two words scribbled on it: the name of the house they were heading for. Without further direction or guidance, they were left on their own. The helicopter took off, and as the thud of its rotor blades gradually faded into the distance, the two colleagues suddenly realized that it was dark, cold, wet and misty, that they didn't know where they were – and that their business suits were just about the most unsuitable clothing imaginable for their surroundings.

Still, being enterprising people, they pressed on. Eventually a road came in sight, and they hailed a distant figure to ask for directions to their destination. Simple enough, you might think – except that the passer-by replied in what sounded like French, and since neither of them was exactly fluent in that language, even a simple enquiry was much more difficult than they had expected. But they carried on, and their persistence eventually paid off. Several hours later, exhausted, soaked to the skin, and with their business suits torn and ragged, they arrived at the place where the course was to be held, ready for a long, hot bath and a good sleep. But the organizers had other ideas. By now it was 6.00 a.m. and they were up bright and early, ready for a prompt start to the day. Of course, *they* hadn't spent the previous night tramping through woods and across mountains! But then, they didn't need to, because they had already achieved a state of 'enlightenment'.

As the weary and bedraggled course participants staggered in two by two, they were each presented with a small parcel. What did this parcel contain? A crystal. As the first session got going, the reasoning behind it all was unfolded. 'This course is quite unlike any course you have ever been on before,' they were told. You could say that again! 'Instead of merely treating the symptoms of bad management, this time we are going right back to fundamentals: to you as a manager, and to your own personal worldview and lifestyle. For a start, why did you arrive here in such a mess, and take so long to make it?' Some of them had an answer for that – but decided that the opening session was not the best time to throw abusive comments at the organizers. But when they heard the 'real' answer some of them began to wonder if they were dreaming. 'The problem is that you've been brought up and trained to think and live in all the wrong ways. To put it simply, you're too left-brained. Too rationalistic, mechanistic and logical in your attitude towards problem-solving. If only you were more right-brained, more intuitive, more open, more spiritually aware and more in tune with your environment, you'd have made it here right away. And instead of being angry, you'd have been able to handle your emotions and to relate positively both to yourself and to other people.'

As one day followed another, the term 'New Age' was used with ever-increasing frequency to describe the philosophy behind this process of re-education. What is wrong with industry? Answer: its managers are locked into a 'machine age' mentality. A mind-set which assumes that people are like machines, and that the job of the manager is to press the right buttons so that the machines work in the proper way. In fact, of course, we all know that people are not like that, so is it surprising if chaos and disintegration result from this sort of attitude? But why did anyone ever imagine that things did work like this? Answer: because in the bad old days, people used to think that way about God. God was the supreme machine-minder, pressing buttons to make the world – and its people – work in the ways God wanted. How then can we break out of this negative and self-defeating view of the world and move on into the 'systems age', which takes full account of the total world structure and in which people see themselves in their proper place? Answer: by abandoning the traditional western Christian view of God, in favour of a holistic view of things in which people and God are made of the same stuff – indeed, are the same stuff. And the crystal? That is a source of cosmic 'God-energy', from which the modern manager can receive the power to undergo such a far-reaching transformation of consciousness.

Not surprisingly, some of the managers found all this a bit threatening – especially those with a traditional Christian conviction. Others found themselves uneasy without being able to identify the precise reasons. As a result, there were many lasting repercussions for the company that organized the training – as there have been in other places around the world. Mere unease has frequently given way to litigation and wide-ranging claims about brainwashing and the violation of human rights.

SOME COMMON THREADS

We will look at all these issues in greater depth in subsequent chapters. But the four stories we have looked at highlight some key aspects of the New Age Movement. Though each incident is quite unique, and the channeling of messages from extraterrestrials might seem light-years away from business management, there are some fundamental connexions. Adrian Van Leen, a self-styled 'cult buster' from Australia, identifies three major beliefs that run through all aspects of New Age thinking:

- 'All is one.' What historians of religion would call 'monism'. That is, the belief that reality consists of one basic substance, and that ultimately there is no difference between a rock, a person or a carrot.
- 'All is "God".' That is, 'pantheism': 'God' is an impersonal energy or force and, as such, permeates everything.
- 'Humanity needs a change in consciousness.' This is where the various techniques and therapies come into the picture. Once these are tapped correctly by a large enough number of people, the whole of humanity will be moved onto a new level of consciousness.

The two catchwords, transformation and consciousness, are central to all that the New Age stands for. New Agers are acutely aware of the fact that the world is in a mess, that people are in a mess, both individually and together, and that things must change. Their agenda invariably includes personal transformation, social transformation, global transformation and – ultimately – cosmic transformation. To put it simply we have got things wrong and we must now get things right. In order to do this we must change our present habits and ways of thinking, and thus reach a new level of consciousness. This is not just an intellectual understanding of how things are, but includes actually becoming a part of the cosmos, and feeling at one with that great universal consciousness which is peopled by extraterrestrials and other spiritual beings, and is also united with the energy fields of the earth and all that is in them. This is the point at which the crystals given to managers join forces with channeled entities such as Ramtha, Michael and the rest, while experiences like rebirthing become a means to the psychological and metaphysical end of discovering one's own true identity and place within the universal scheme of things. It is widely believed that we have now entered a new – and final – stage in the evolution of the human race. No longer will impersonal forces 'choose' by the process of natural selection those individuals best suited to survive. Rather, now evolution can become conscious, and we can learn both to control and to direct it. As Marilyn Ferguson puts it, 'if we realize that we are part of a dynamic system, one in which any action affects the whole, we are empowered to change it . . . Each of us is – potentially – the difference in the world.'[11] We are all interconnected not only with one another, but also as parts of some greater cosmic consciousness, and for that reason we will all ultimately be overtaken by it. But it is better to be enlightened, realize what is going on, and get involved as soon as possible. Hence the great popularity of therapies and techniques that can induce a change of personal consciousness, and enable us to get in tune with the great world Soul, to live at peace with ourselves because we are at one with the cosmos.

All this is radically different from mainstream Christian belief. The New Age has no place for sin. Nor can it accommodate a Jesus who is in any sense a definitive revelation of the character of God: in the words of Kenneth Wapnick, he is 'one of God's helpers'.[12] At a theological level, the New Age is clearly a major challenge to traditional Christianity. But its challenge runs deeper than that. For it also apparently has the power to address the needs of women and men in today's world in a way that the Church has long since lost. Many serious spiritual searchers are finding the Church's answers to their questions ever less convincing, and the

New Age alternatives ever more attractive. For that reason alone, Western Christians should pay careful attention to it.

My friend was right: the New Age *is* 'the sweepings of the ages'. Some of the terminology has changed, as the New Age has to some extent adopted a scientific and technological outlook. But for all that, there is nothing very new in the New Age. In fact, that is one of its attractions: it has the power to pick up elements from all places and all ages, and transform them into a message of new power and relevance for modern people. Why it has happened at this time in history is the next mystery we must try to unravel.

Chapter 2

WHAT IS THE NEW AGE?

*F*EELING lost already? With such a diverse assortment of spiritual goodies on sale at the New Age store, most customers visiting for the first time find themselves totally mesmerized by it all. Even those who call in regularly find the dazzling display very difficult to describe to others. Understanding the New Age is like trying to wrestle with a jelly. As soon as you think you've got it all under control, the shape of the whole thing changes and you have to start again. For many people, that is precisely its attraction. There is so much to explore that you can never get bored. New Agers would certainly have no trouble agreeing with the eighteenth-century British poet William Cowper, who once wrote

> *Variety's the very spice of life*
> *That gives it all its flavour.*

In fact, by his definition of the 'flavour' of life, the New Age must be just about the hottest concoction around. It gives a spiritual searcher the freedom to choose from a whole range of possibilities, without necessarily making a specific commitment to any of them. Here, as elsewhere, fashions and fads come and go. A typical New Age

searcher will become fascinated by, let us say, the
mysticism of the Sufis, and that will last for a while.
Then he or she will move on to certain forms of healing
therapy or physical bodywork – something like Reiki,
aromatherapy, acupuncture or Rolfing, pe   Reincarnation might then suddenly become the   of
the month. Then the searcher may progress to past-life
recall therapies and become an avid consumer of
writings allegedly 'channeled' from entities in   me
other world. Because books of this kind often in e
references to Jesus, you can also expect to discover
various Christian beliefs being sucked in and added to
this heady mixture of pop spirituality.

No matter what your needs may be, you can almost
certainly find somebody somewhere who will have the
answer to them. A 1990 ad for the San Francisco
Liberty, Truth and Love Event invited participants
to 'Choose to experience true love; pure truth; total
liberty; all-planetary authority; universal victorious
power; immortality; eternal life; wisdom, knowledge
and enlightenment; forgiveness, grace, mercy and prosperity; fulfilment, faith, hope and satisfaction; happiness, peace and joy.' With all this – and more – on offer,
the possibilities are obviously endless. So can we ever
pin the New Age Movement down at all? Well, yes and
no. By definition, we can expect that anything called a
'movement' will always be on the move. But at the same
time, it is possible to some extent to document the
emergence of the New Age, and to sketch out some of
its main characteristics.

THE AGE OF AQUARIUS

The New Age is often referred to as the Age of Aquarius
– the peri........hich, on the ancient astrological timetable,
will........... the Age of Pisces, in which we are now
liv..............major characteristics of our own age are
most........ings which would be better forgotten – division,
war........ justice, hatred, mistrust and bigotry. All of them
thi........ that, it is claimed, were ultimately related to
t.........paration between God and humanity that was
demanded by organized religion. By contrast, the Age of
Aquarius, when it dawns, will be a time of peace,
harmony, wholeness and restoration – for people, and
ultimately for the whole universe. A time when people
and God will be reunified, when there will be a healing of
all the separation and an assertion of the fact that we are
all part of our natural environment. As a result, the New
Age is not about domination or competition, but about
co-operation. People are looking to see where they
belong, where they connect with other aspects of the
cosmos. In the process they are discovering that we are
not actually at the mercy of objective forces arraigned
against us out there – the only real energy is within
ourselves. And the only reality we experience is what we
create ourselves. So if we all create our own reality, then
by focusing on wholeness and health, instead of worrying
about disasters and failures, we can together create
something entirely new, that will be better than what has
gone before. Back in 1987, *New Age Journal* conducted a
reader survey in which people were invited to give their
definitions of the coming New Age. One person
described it as 'ultimately a vision of a world transformed,
a heaven on earth, a society in which the problems of
today are overcome and a new existence emerges.'

Another wrote of 'moving into an era that emphasizes self-discovery, spiritual growth, and enlightenment.'[1] The agenda is still the same today, though if anything it has become more self-consciously spiritual. When the *San Francisco Chronicle*'s 'Question Man' asked people in July 1990, 'What is the New Age all about?' one of the answers he got said: 'It's a conscious raising of the world – who we are and why we're here. New Age music is for meditating to get in touch with your higher self and spiritual guides. These ideas have been here since the beginning of time, but now more people who are old souls are raising the consciousness of the whole. Having raised themselves affects the whole.'[2] So now you know!

The idea got its first mass exposure back in the sixties, with the rock musical *Hair* and its popular theme song, 'This is the Age of Aquarius', which defined it as 'the age of the mind's true liberation'. But it was not until the late 1980s that the New Age Movement became widely known as a way in which people could prepare themselves for this coming age of enlightenment and personal fulfilment. Like any cultural movement, it did not come from nowhere, and many of its elements had been around for a long time before that. As long ago as 1907 a book called *The Aquarian Gospel of Jesus Christ* had promoted a similar idea. But public awareness has grown noticeably in the last five years. Academics like Marilyn Ferguson and Hollywood stars like Shirley Maclaine have had enormous influence through their books and public pronouncements on the subject. At the same time, management consultants have spread the New Age message across the corporate world of business executives. And the environmental movement has brought the whole world of New Age spirituality to many who would never have thought of themselves as religious, let alone mystics. When the UK Green Party held its first annual conference at Easter 1989, journalists and political commentators were spellbound as they watched delegates begin each day with an act of 'attunement' to Gaia. Some ridiculed it – most simply had no idea what was going on. But at least no one could miss it.

So what is it that holds all these apparently contrasting strands together? Simply, the common vision of the arrival of a New Age of enlightenment and harmony – predicted to dawn sometime between now and the year 2062 – perhaps heralded by the arrival of a messiah-figure, Maitreya. Anyone can see that there is a growing sense of anticipation and excitement, a feeling that things cannot continue like they are for much longer. And there is a conviction that the end of the century – which will also be the end of the millenium – will be a momentous occasion in the whole of human history. If we are to break free from the mistakes of the past, many things will have to change – not least the attitudes and outlook of people and institutions. A paradigm shift will have to take place, in which we will look at ourselves and our world in a holistic way rather than through the fragmentation that has brought so much misery in the past; a paradigm shift that will open people's minds to new possibilities. In particular, there will have to be a changed outlook that will break away from the bad habits of the past and will have an open-ended commitment to discovering new ways for the future; an outlook that will recognize the basic frustration that modern western culture has created, and which will enable people to explore other dimensions of existence and experience, while building on the insights of modern science. In a word, there will have to be a move away from rationalist materialism towards a more mystical world of the spirit, in which people will be able actually to experience a new way of life for themselves. As the British aristocrat Sir George Trevelyan puts it: 'We are approaching a crucial turning point . . . Much may have to fall away in our present social structures, but a new society may then emerge in which the unifying spiritual impulse is genuinely at work.'[3]

It is in this context that anything offering the possibility of a change in human outlook is being seized upon with great enthusiasm. Elements from eastern mysticism combine with modern psychoanalysis, meditation techniques and holistic health to produce a complex maze of pathways to personal fulfilment and wholeness. Alongside this interest in personal transformation, the insights of political movements that are pressing for social change can also be incorporated – hence the popularity among New Agers of well-known organizations like Amnesty International, Greenpeace and Friends of the Earth, and of lesser-known movements such as Pulse of the Planet and the Peace Navy. For the most part, these organizations would not describe themselves as 'New Age'. Some of them have been around for a long time, and it is not always easy to see what logical connexion they might have with the New Age Movement. But this is typical of how the New Age networks operate. Everything works by association, without any apparent need to systematize it or make it hang together. Anything and everything that has potential for promoting a change of thinking among the world's people will be sucked up and utilized as we move relentlessly towards the Age of Aquarius. The only consideration that determines a thing's value – whether it be a large organization or a personal spiritual technique – is its usefulness in promoting transformation, on a personal or global or cosmic scale. How such a transformation will be brought about is still uncertain. As the historian William Irwin Thompson says in his book *From Nation to Emancipation*, 'Whether the movement from one world system to another will involve stumbling or total collapse may very well depend on the success or failure of the new age movement . . .'[4]

Faced with such uncertainty, some New Agers are setting up separate communities to ensure their own safety through the coming world trauma. Hundreds of people have bought real estate in Yelm, a farming hamlet south of Seattle, in order to be close to J. Z. Knight and the cosmic wisdom of Ramtha. In Montana, the Ides of March 1990 saw thousands of members of the New Age Church Universal and Triumphant crawling into forty-five underground bunkers at a place called Glastonbury, just north of Yellowstone National Park, in a chilling dummy run of doomsday. This was not the first time the leader of this group, Elizabeth Clare Prophet, had predicted that the end would arrive. The same people had expected it back in 1987, and again in April and December 1989. It obviously hasn't come yet, but that doesn't stop them continuing to buy their own underground shelters at $13,000 a time, largely because Prophet has managed to convince them that the Ascended Masters who gav her the information changed their minds as a result of the 'decreeing' (rapid chanting) of the group's members.

This was but one of the latest in a whole string of events designed to enhance spiritual awareness across the globe. The most heavily publicized was the universal 'Harmonic Convergence' on 16–17 August 1987, when New Agers gathered at hundreds of sacred sites all over the world, from England's Stonehenge to California's Mount Shasta, from the Great Pyramid of Cheops in Egypt to the top of the Andes in Peru. The purpose of it all was to 'synchronize the Earth with the rest of the galaxy', and the organizer, Jose Arguelles, announced that 'great, unprecedented outpourings of extraterrestrial intelligence . . . will be clearly received'. Basing his calculations on various Mayan and Aztec astrological predictions, Arguelles – who holds a PhD from Chicago University – saw this great festival of shamanic chanting, drumming and meditation as the point at which the world's values would begin to change. In his article in *Life Times Magazine* he predicted that this process would end by 1992, when 'the phase shift transiting civilization from a military state of terror to a deindustrialized, decentralized, post-military planetary society will be complete at least in its foundations . . .'⁵ The pre-event publicity declared that 'The call is out for 144,000 Rainbow Humans to gather at sacred sites all over the earth for the two days from sunrise August 16th to sunrise August 18th,' promising that 'Energy will flow through the linked network of sacred sites . . . as we learn to become co-creators and friends with God.' Unfortunately, it did not quite work out that way: only 20,000 people turned out, and many of them were disappointed by the outcome. As a result, today's New Agers are likely to be somewhat more cautious in their claims and predictions. But there are still many thousands of spiritual pilgrims who regularly congregate with the same mood of expectancy at sacred sites around the world.

ORIGINS

To understand the origins of all this, come with me on a whirlwind tour of the last 500 years of western history and culture. For it is no coincidence that the New Age

Movement has emerged as we head towards the start of a new millenium, after a period of immense change in world civilization. Change is nothing new: it has been a way of life in the West for half a millenium and more. Beginning right back with the great European explorers in the fourteenth and fifteenth centuries, there has been a non-stop explosion of knowledge that has radically affected the whole way in which we live and think. Prior to that, life was a pretty simple affair. It was not easy, for in medieval Europe life expectancy was low, the chance of economic advancement was non-existent for most, and merely to exist was an uphill struggle. But in spite of such hardship, people had a simple view by which to make sense of it all. The earth was a flat disc. Underneath was the world of the dead. Up aloft was heaven. Civilization was mostly concentrated around the shores of the Mediterranean Sea. Global confrontation was generally limited to petty skirmishes between local tyrants.

As long as God was up in heaven, all was well. And keeping God there was merely a matter of doing the right things in the right places at the right times. Religion permeated the whole of life. For peasant farmers, sowing seeds and other agricultural operations had religious overtones. For politicians, national strategies were invariably bound up with religious observance. Though there were no doubt many discontinuities and tensions in such a life, everyone shared more or less the same worldview and lived with the same set of settled expectations.

But such a world could not last for ever. Nor did it. First came the explorers. People in the European heartlands had known for a long time of the existence of other countries seemingly more esoteric and mystical than their own. In particular, the Bible lands at the eastern end of the Mediterranean had always been places of pilgrimage for those who could afford to go – and some of the bravest European warriors had lost their lives in futile battles for possession of these places. But the possibility of travel to such foreign parts soon inspired others with dreams of lands even more remote. As Spanish and Portuguese navigators looked over the Atlantic Ocean towards the setting sun, they wondered what they might find beyond the horizon. And it was only a matter of time before they determined to test the reality of their theories by embarking on long and dangerous sea journeys. Many did not survive. But those who made it back to their homelands carried with them souvenirs of strange and distant places, and told hair-raising tales that only served to inspire others to join this exciting enterprise for themselves. The revelation that Europe was only a small part of the world came as a great shock to some and provided a major impetus to others who, while lacking the skills and opportunity to discover new lands, threw themselves with great energy into the search for new light on other hitherto unknown aspects of our world. If so much of the world was yet to be discovered, how could we be certain about anything? Was the earth really a flat disc? Was it really the centre of the universe? And if not, what was the truth about it all? Were humans really different from animals? And was it necessary to believe in a God wiser than mere mortals in order to make sense of it all?

It was only a matter of time before there began to emerge answers so startling that leading European thinkers realized that they were not just engaged in a search for personal enlightenment: they were caught up in a movement so vast and exciting that they were soon talking of it as *the* Enlightenment. The changes in human

knowledge and understanding that took place at this time
were so far-reaching that it seemed as if all that had gone
before had been total darkness compared with the great
light that was now dawning. People began to see the
world through new eyes, and from different perspectives.
Nothing would ever be the same again.

New discoveries were made at breathtaking speed.
Barriers began to fall in every area of human understanding. It came to be taken for granted that, contrary to
ancient belief, the world was not a flat disc but a round
globe. Copernicus reformulated our entire understanding of the workings of the universe. Isaac Newton
lay in an orchard reflecting on why apples always fall
down and not up – and thought of the concept of gravity
to explain it. Scientists formulated 'laws of nature' that
gave a coherent explanation of many things that had
previously seemed semi-miraculous. In due course
others began to develop medical science, with its great
potential for understanding how the body works, and
for actually improving its performance and offering
enhanced vitality and life expectancy to all. And
hard on the heels of all this progress came the
Industrial Revolution, the development of technology
and the invention of modern forms of transportation.
Inevitably, as new worlds were opened up, the developing
European thinking was spread far beyond the continent
in which it originated. And so was born that phenomenon
which we now call 'western culture': a total worldview
and way of life that would ultimately – for good or ill –
leave no part of the world wholly untouched by its
influence.

These must have been exciting times in which to live.
Great technological advances were being made, and
enormous changes in the way in which people under-

stood the world and its inhabitants were taking place. Gone were the days when people turned to superstition and mythology – and religion – as a means of unravelling life's mysteries. In fact, they soon concluded that these were the very things that had kept people in ignorance for so long. For the source of all these new ideas that catapulted humanity from the medieval world into the modern age was not some esoteric revelation from another plane of existence. It had all come about simply and solely as human beings had thought long and hard about the world and its workings, and had come up with cool, calculated, logical – and therefore 'scientific' – answers. They didn't always get it right first time, of course. But even then, the systematic and patient testing of conflicting hypotheses and theories usually won through to the truth in the end. It seemed as if there was nothing that the trained, intelligent human person could not do.

In due course, even the barriers of the physical world itself were broken, and a man was sent into space. When Yuri Gagarin returned from his historic space flight in 1961, and proudly declared that he had seen no sign of God up there, many people felt that was a fitting epitaph for any kind of religious worldview. Given the time, money and expertise, nothing now seemed impossible. When scientists could give precise answers to all the questions, who needed God as a means of explaining things? The answer seemed obvious: no one. And in so far as religion would survive in the modern world, it could only ever be a prop for people who in various ways were considered intellectually substandard and psychologically inadequate.

At least, that's how it all seemed thirty years ago. Religion – especially the traditional Christianity of the western world – had every appearance of being in a state of terminal decline. As long ago as 1883 the German philosopher Friedrich Nietzsche had coined the slogan 'God is dead', and by the mid-sixties of the twentieth century several Christian theologians were ready to agree with him. The traditional idea of God had, of course, been under threat for quite some time, not so much from non-Christian rationalist thinkers as from Christians who had tried to redefine their faith by reference to rationalist categories.

Back in the eighteenth century, earnest believers had sought to defend the Bible from the attacks of rationalist historians who saw it not as a special book at all, but as a document just like any other of its times. One of the leading Christians in this debate was the great German theologian, Friedrich Schleiermacher (1768–1834). Fired by a genuine desire to protect religious belief from the onslaughts of people whom he regarded as infidels and atheists, he came up with a definition of belief that placed it beyond the reach of reason altogether. True faith, he claimed, was quite different from things like behaviour or science. Religion was all about pure feeling – and by definition, that could never be subjected to thoroughgoing intellectual analysis. That being the case, it would not really matter what rationalist historians made of the Bible and other apparently tangible manifestations of faith, for they could never get to the heart of the matter by that route.

Schleiermacher's distinction between the world of science and reason and the world of religion was so widely accepted by Christians that he came to be known as 'the father of modern theology'. And it led to what many outside the churches regarded as a kind of spiritual schizophrenia on the part of those still in them. For it meant that Christian scholars could approach the historical and literary aspects of Christianity in a thoroughly rationalistic way, while still preserving some sort of belief in God – but a God who could never be understood by reference to the very standards and values which they themselves both believed in and practised! And so the Church, along with other cultural institutions in the West, was swallowed up by the new, self-confident, all-pervading worldview dominated by the progress of science, reason, technology and materialism. A factor which goes some considerable way towards explaining why the western Church is in such bad shape today.

Yuri Gagarin's space flight around the earth seemed at the time to be symbolic of technology's coming of age, but storm-clouds were then gathering which would in the following thirty years radically change the contours of much of the western cultural landscape. Looking back, we can now see that the message of the 'death of God' theologians of the sixties was more of an epitaph for western Enlightenment culture than one for religion. For religious belief in the broadest sense is experiencing a vigorous revival today. Clayton Carlson is the senior vice-president of one of America's largest publishing houses. When we met at his office, which is in a trendy part of San Francisco's waterfront area not far from Fisherman's Wharf, he reflected on his own experience. A quarter of a century before, as a young man, he had begun his career in New York. Most people moving to the big cities of the east coast at that time came from traditional backgrounds in small towns, where going to church was one of the ways of showing you were a good, solid citizen. But to make progress in the 'high culture' of Manhattan, they generally repressed all that, because it was widely regarded as irrelevant. 'If you were interested in religious things,' commented Carlson, 'it was somehow subcultural – certainly a symbol of psychological weakness. But today? That has gone. Absolutely gone. If anything, it is *avant garde* to be religious. Overall in the culture now, the openness to the spirit is just enormous.' As a publisher he should know, for evangelical Christian publications now account for more than a third of all US commercial book sales, while New Age books are the fastest growing sector of the market throughout the world.

Any visitor to contemporary California can see what he means. The whole place is just buzzing with mystical awareness – coupled with a serious spiritual search for new answers to the human predicament. Why else would leading figures from many walks of life put their reputations on the line by openly publicizing their experiences of the spirit world? Relaxing in his Walnut Creek home, Ron Valle, transpersonal psychologist and former professor at Orinda's John F. Kennedy University, put it to me this way: 'I think there's a basic frustration in all of us. The mystery of God, the mystery of awe, has been taken away – at least for the lay person – by science. There's no room in our culture for that kind of experience we all long for. We're starving spiritually.' In that final sentence he encapsulated what today's new spiritual search is all about. Despite all the science, all the technology, all the institutions and expertise, modern western people still have a gap in their lives. As people look at their everyday lifestyles – shopping, work, education, recreation – many ask what the purpose of it all might be. Though it is not easy to articulate, they have a gut feeling that the quality of life is getting worse all the time, and that all the scientific, technological and social change of the last two hundred years is getting us nowhere. Somewhere along the line, some fundamental human and spiritual values have been lost. In a 1978 interview with the *New York Times*, Zbigniew Brzezinski, then chairman of the US Security Council, sensed an 'increasing yearning for something spiritual' among people who, materially at least, appeared to have it all made for them.[6] Now, little more than a decade later, millions of westerners would agree with him. Ever-increasing numbers of thinking people are reaching the conclusion that our world is in such a mess precisely because we have lost touch with spiritual meaning. Faced with a world that seems to be spinning out of control, with the planet itself choking to death on industrial pollution, millions of people are clearly searching for something sacred, and are desperate to find spiritual satisfaction in a consumerist world.

MODERN CHALLENGES

How and why has this happened? Simple questions rarely have straightforward answers. And this one is no exception. But we can say one thing without hesitation. The New Age Movement is a response to the acknowledged failure of the scientific and materialist worldview to deliver the goods. The great Enlightenment vision of a better world for everyone has simply not materialized. Not only has the fundamental human predicament not improved, but as the twentieth century has progressed things have actually got worse. What is more, the increasing pane of change, and the accompanying difficulties of keeping up with it, are hitting people everywhere – in the workplace and in the family, as well as on the global and international scene. Things are happening today that, quite simply, have never happened before in the whole of time. For instance, take the speed at which we can now travel and communicate. It has increased more in our own generation than in every other generation there has ever been! That is a simple example. But it is symptomatic of what is now taking place at every level of human existence. Who in the early 1980s would have believed that by the end of the decade Communism could have collapsed so totally in eastern Europe – and done so almost literally overnight? Of course, change is nothing new. But up until the modern era, things tended to change only slowly, and that meant that people were able to adapt quite easily as part of a naturally evolving process. But the faster the pace of change, the more difficult it is to handle. Solutions to problems are likely to be redundant long before they have been worked out. The world is moving on all the time, and that means we are likely to fall further and further behind in coping with things. No wonder, then, that these increasing pressures are directing us to a reappraisal of some of the most basic questions of all. Matters that our grandparents thought had been settled for all time are now up for debate again – questions about the world and its systems, about life and its meaning, about people and their relationships, about values and religion. And, in general, westerners are becoming less and less satisfied with the traditional answers of their culture.

Western science and technology have produced many benefits, which it would be impossible – and foolish – to deny. Modern medical science must surely have improved the lifestyle of most of us, and the development of efficient worldwide transportation systems has done much to open our eyes to the global dimensions of our own lives. But the course of progress has not run smoothly. A hundred years ago, it was confidently believed that through evolution the human race was getting better all the time. But early in the twentieth century this particular notion was dealt a death blow by one of the most savage and bloody conflicts ever seen in world history. This was followed not long afterwards by a second great world war. And even though some aspects of international relations may seem to have changed for the better today, the world is still a brutal place for most of its people, as the 1991 Gulf War has depicted so graphically. Michael Murphy is the founder and chairman of the Esalen Institute at Big Sur, California, one of the world's biggest and longest-established personal growth centres. He speaks for many when he says, 'Science, while it is wonderful, has outlived a lot of its promises. Not many still say technology is going to bring us incredible happiness. There's a renewed interest in the contemplative and meditative, in the living spirit of God, among orthodox Catholics, Buddhists, agnostics and New Agers.'

Some of the fruits of modern science and technology have had a decidedly bitter-sweet taste. Who could have forseen that the advances of science would mostly be used to present us with ever more terrifying ways of annihilating one another? Who could have imagined that improving standards of health care, leading to longer life expectancy and falling infant mortality, would enable the world's population to increase to the point where many nations are constantly on a knife-edge between survival and extinction? Who could have predicted that the efficient use of fertilizers and pesticides to produce more food for this expanding population would lead to the pollution of the world's water, one of its most precious resources? How could anyone have guessed that the development of modern transportation systems, and the fuels used to operate them, would lead to the depletion of the ozone layer? That may be a catastrophe that could yet see us all fried alive in our own lifetime. And even if that doesn't happen, the unprecedented number of volcanic eruptions and earthquakes in recent years – not to mention unpredictable climatic changes – has convinced many people that something funny is happening to the world on which we all depend.

Moreover, there are an enormous number of people in western society who for one reason or another have lost faith in their institutions, and have decided that the remaining structures are concerned mainly for their own survival and welfare as institutions. Mistrust and cynicism are the order of the day. At one time medical doctors, with their strict Hippocratic oath and their commitment to other people's welfare, were highly regarded as the least corruptible profession of all. Today they are widely viewed with suspicion as people more interested in patient hours and covering their overheads than in the health and welfare of those whom they treat. And even those patients who are not quite so cynical still find themselves drawn to alternative therapies and holistic health techniques, simply because the professional medic no longer has enough time to deal adequately with the needs of every single patient.

Establishment religion fares no better. The churches have always been unsure about Enlightenment rationalism, but they have generally adopted it by default as their own dominant worldview. They are now in the process of suffering the consequences. As a result, many who are on the fringes of organized religion have come to believe that any spiritual reality there once was has been syphoned off or suppressed in the interests of the bureaucratic establishment, and that the professional clergy are so concerned with keeping the machinery going and maintaining their own power and position that they have lost touch with any kind of movement of the spirit. There is a widespread feeling that if the mystical side of religion is to be rediscovered, it will not be in the mainstream establishment, but on the fringes – whether in charismatic forms of Christianity or in the transformational therapies of the New Age Movement. The literature of the New Age Universal 'Christianity without Religion' movement, based in the Canary Islands, expresses the feelings of many people: 'You owe it to your God to stay away from organized institutionalized man-made religion . . . Empty prayer in empty churches is noise . . . You can become a living church *without* religion, so act now – serve God, not man!'

Whether all this is a wholly accurate analysis of western culture is not our concern just now. The fact is that enough people believe it for it to have a significant impact. It seems that we have not been able to change or improve the world even by our own best efforts. The Enlightenment dream has turned into a nightmare. But the dream will not go away. People still aspire to a better life. A life in which we can live in harmony with one another, at peace with our planet and in tune with ourselves. The longing for a 'New Age' is deeply rooted in the human heart. And if traditional western materialist routes to personal fulfilment and transformation are blocked, then we must have been looking in the wrong direction.

That is another basic assumption of most New Agers. They conclude that somewhere after the Enlightenment some genuine spiritual values and insights got lost. Because of the dominance of rationalism and reasonableness, the current establishment options are therefore pale remnants of the spiritual fire that started them all – and to recover a sense of our own destiny and purpose, we need to get back to the fire again. In the effort to do so, mystical traditions of the past such as Gnosticism or Kabbalah Judaism rub shoulders with the speculations of modern science fiction, much of which also has a mystical and spiritual character. In the search for ultimate answers, people will as readily look to the shamans of native North American religion as to visitors from other planets. Things that were being dismissed as superstitious and mythology a generation ago are now projected onto the centre stage as the key to the meaning of life's mysteries, as foreign and ancient traditions are re-examined for possible contact with some kind of metaphysical wisdom. When Joseph Campbell presented a series on the mythical traditions of eastern religions for the American PBS network, the whole nation stopped to watch, fascinated with all these wonderful tales and the sense of mystery that they invoke. Almost overnight, the ancient mysteries have become the way to get things straight.

Many reactionary movements operate in this way, taking it for granted that the stranger a thing is, the more authentic it is likely to be. So it is no surprise that many modern spiritual searchers take it for granted that truth is some kind of mystical, secret thing which the institutions of modern society have buried in order to preserve their own vested interests. We can see this quite clearly in the way so many people eagerly embrace alternative practices in areas like medicine, health and education, as well as in the more narrowly defined religious realm. As a result, anything that seems to be coming from another place – preferably ancient and non-western – has a running start. Clayton Carlson again: 'When I started being interested in this, the major issue was credulity. People had difficulty in believing. Now the problem is incredulity –

people will in reaction believe anything.' But not quite anything. For in one of those strange ironies which characterize much of the New Age Movement, it is also claimed that modern science points in the same direction. Put simply, it was the old science of people like Newton that led us into a blind alley, with its insistence on unchangeable 'laws of nature' and its assumption that things work on a cause-and-effect basis like well-oiled machinery. But the new science developed largely under the influence of Albert Einstein has shown that things are not like that. Even matter itself may not be as solid as it seems, but could just be one manifestation of the energy that runs through everything in the universe. New Age scientists are not slow to jump to that conclusion, and readily identify the dynamic viewpoint of modern physics with the age-old belief of eastern religions, that 'God', people and the earth itself are all merely different aspects of the one cosmic reality.

In his best-selling book, *The Turning Point*, Fritjof Capra, professor of physics at the University of California in Berkeley, observes:

> The new concepts in physics have brought about a profound change in our world view; from the mechanistic conception of Descartes and Newton to a holistic or ecological view, a view which I have found to be similar to the views of mystics of all ages and traditions.[7]

IDENTIFYING THE NEW AGERS

Who are the people most attracted by all this? Dissatisfaction with the establishment is nothing new in the recent history of western culture. Back in the sixties, such feelings surfaced through radical student movements and the whole hippy phenomenon. There are some connexions with all that, but it is difficult to trace the New Age Movement's origins exclusively back to those groups. The protestors of the sixties were almost entirely young people, whereas today's New Age Movement cuts across all age groups. Moreover, the protest movement of the sixties was often bound up with the use of drugs and with anti-establishment lifestyles. But today's New Agers are more likely to be found living quietly in suburbia, with the same trappings of prosperity and success as everyone else. They are mechanics, engineers, police chiefs, psychologists, teachers – and scientists. Which is why Stephen Dunning of the University of Pennsylvania can brand the New Age as 'a yuppie version of spirituality'.

Of course, the people who are living in the suburbs today were the kids of the sixties. Through the seventies and most of the eighties they were busy raising their families, and by the start of the nineties they had reached that stage which is often called mid-life crisis. At a certain point in life, usually when they've made it – or come to terms with the fact that they're not going to go any further – people have the leisure to indulge in the luxury that is speculation. Religion has been on the back-burner for twenty to thirty years while they have got on with the more serious business of making money and creating a comfortable lifestyle. But once they have achieved those goals, quite a few try to rediscover their spiritual roots, or start for the first time to read serious psychological material, or delve into the great classics of ancient literature and philosophy.

Traditionally, the religious roots that such people went to were to be found in the Christian church. In the past they frequently turned to it at times of crisis or uncertainty. When America was changing from an agricultural to an industrial society back in the mid-1700s, the transformation was accompanied by what has been called the Great Religious Awakening. Nearer to our own time, in the 1950s, following the war, people in America (though not in Britain) went back to church in a big way. But those who grew up in the 1960s have a different outlook on life. For a whole variety of reasons – immigration, greater global awareness, dissatisfaction with Christianity – they are more conscious of the fact that going back to church is not the only way to find new meaning in life. There is a wide range of options out there just waiting to be explored, most of them a good deal more appealing than Establishment Christianity. For while Christianity seems to encapsulate all the weaknesses of western culture, New Age thinking claims to encompass what is good and transform it into something even better.

It is not a drug-based counter-culture, but it can easily endorse and build on the experiences of expanded consciousness of those who took LSD back in the sixties, promoting them as part of a much larger, more serious search for spiritual meaning.

The 'new science' has also been widely applauded by the New Age Movement and eagerly incorporated into its orbit. Thus the Movement can offer a spiritual basis for living without also rejecting those very aspects of modern technology which have produced the creature comforts we all like to enjoy.

And the New Age is the ultimate fulfilment of the Great American Dream. It is not accidental that it should all have started in California. The United States itself, and the west coast in particular, has always been perceived as the place to make a new start. Free from the inhibitions, weaknesses and failures of the past, the New Age dream presents ever more attractive possibilities for a change and transformation that can encompass every aspect of life – from the acquisition of a new body through plastic surgery and healthy diets – to the realization of some of the more esoteric elements of American national consciousness. American New Agers often draw attention to the fact that – unlike the European cultural heritage – their whole society has a distinctively mystical foundation. A majority of the leaders of the American Revolution were personally connected with mystical traditions – a fact that ordinary citizens are reminded of every day. For not only does the Great Seal declare on its reverse that 'A New Order of the Ages Begins', but the familiar greenback dollar bill combines symbols drawn from Rosicrucian, Masonic and Hermetic traditions. In her book *The Aquarian Conspiracy*, Marilyn Ferguson writes of the New Age Movement as 'the second American revolution', claiming that 'American society has at hand most of the factors that could bring about collective transformation: relative freedom, relative tolerance, affluence enough to be disillusioned with affluence, achievements enough to know that something different is needed.'[8]

Viewed from this angle, it is tempting to see the New Age Movement as yet another example of the kind of outmoded drum-beating nationalism that has led us into the present confrontational world situation which New Agers claim to dislike so much. The Movement might be seen as a more subtle form of imperialism for a post-colonial world. Not a political imperialism, for that would be impractical, but an intellectual imperialism which claims that everyone else thinks the wrong way and must be brought into line in the cause of justice, peace, harmony and wholeness. The classic line taken by empire-builders since the very beginning of time.

There can be no question that some New Agers fall into that category, and speak freely of bringing about one great world consciousness in which everyone will be the same. But we should not dismiss such talk as merely another imperialistic conspiracy, doomed to go the way of all other such schemes. We need to take New Age thinking more seriously than that. It is not a passing phase, a fashion that will fade away. As we approach the year 2000, many people have a gut feeling that this is a crucial turning point in time. The vision of the Age of Aquarius is one that appeals to the natural aspirations of human beings, and there is a widespread feeling that change is urgently needed. Because the Movement is not a structured organization, the various elements which find themselves sucked into its orbit will no doubt be rearranged and regrouped many times. Some will fall out, others will come in to take their place. The exact shape of the New Age will not be the same in five years as it is today. But whatever shape it adopts, it will be with us for some time, simply because of the fact that it reflects so authentically the needs and the ambitions of western culture today. Our situation is simple. Secular humanism is now largely a spent force. The traditional Judaeo-Christian religion of the western world has all but collapsed. Our culture suffers from a major crisis of confidence, typified by an enormous spiritual vacuum at its centre. Whether New Age thinking will rush in to fill it, only time will tell. Whether it deserves to do so, and what the consequences would be, is a question we must now try and answer.

Chapter 3

'GOING WITHIN'

I HAVE just spent half a day talking about the New Age with a British television producer who is interested in making a few programmes on it. I guess he came to see me to try and get some kind of professional angle on it all. And so we talked, with me mostly describing people I've met, places I've visited and experiences I've had while attending New Age events. I could see he was interested. In fact, he was absolutely captivated by a lot of it, especially the stories of healings and contact with extraterrestrials. But as our conversation progressed, it was just as obvious that he was also mystified by it all, and maybe frustrated because it didn't seem to be fitting into any of his preconceived frameworks for understanding the world and its people. Eventually he came clean and asked the inevitable question that surfaces sooner or later in the minds of most people encountering the New Age for the first time. 'This is all gripping stuff,' he observed, 'but I'm struggling with it. Tell me, what do New Agers actually believe?'

I was ready for that question. In fact, I was surprised it hadn't come sooner. For it has presented itself to me many times as I've worked on this whole phenomenon. I've continually had it in the back of my mind as I've read the mountains of New Age books and pamphlets that have engulfed my desk for the last couple of years. And I've put it directly to people associated with the movement. From Hollywood stars to psychologists, professors and more ordinary practitioners – they all give the same answer. 'New Age is not a belief system. New Age is people who are doing different things that are labelled as that.' The words are those of a Californian therapist, but the sentiments would be widely shared within the movement.

SEARCHING FOR THE SPIRITUAL

When you think about the way it has all come together, it is in any case hard to imagine how such a diverse movement could ever have a systematic statement of beliefs – certainly if you define 'belief' in the traditional western way, where facts and truth claims are of fundamental importance. For most people in the movement simply select elements from many different religious traditions – not for their inherent 'truth', but for their perceived practical usefulness. Wrestling with the meaning of her own spiritual experience, actress Shirley Maclaine comments, 'the thing is, it all seems to be about feeling, not thinking'.[1] A sentiment reinforced by another New Ager who commented that 'Half our mistakes in life arise from feeling where we ought to think, and thinking where we ought to feel.'

You don't need to be a genius to see the point of a statement like that. Traditionally, western culture has always placed a great deal more emphasis on rational thought than on our feelings and emotions. The great Enlightenment thinkers laid so much stress on the importance of human reason and the supremacy of intellectual brain-power in understanding the meaning of everything imaginable, that they almost went so far as to deny that 'truth' could possibly mean anything other than the knowledge of facts. In his speech on 8 August 1968 in which he accepted nomination for the US presidency, Richard Nixon pledged his administration to 'begin by committing ourselves to the truth, to see it like it is and to tell it like it is, to find the truth, to speak the truth and live with the truth. That's what we'll do.' Our whole educational system instils in us the conviction that truth is 'to see it like it is'. It has to do with facts – 'scientific' and rational facts that can be proved by some sort of logical analysis. Therefore beliefs – especially those about the absolutes that religions deal in – must also be related to facts of this same intellectual kind. No doubt that explains why in western Christianity 'belief' has often found its most perfect expression when people give their formal assent to a set of doctrinal or theological propositions. Even to this day, there are many churches around the world in which a mentally handicapped person cannot become a full member, precisely because being a Christian is understood as requiring a certain level of intellectual acceptance of truths and abstract principles.

Hardly surprising, then, that many New Agers – inspired by recent brain and mind research – have come to the conclusion that most westerners are suffering from 'metaphysical amnesia', a condition in which we are rendered incapable of seeing beyond the rational and the reasonable. As a result, they claim, our potential for spiritual fulfilment has been seriously eroded. We have been conditioned to operate through only one half of our brain – the left half, which does the thinking – while the right half, which majors on feeling and perception, has been left undeveloped and immobilized. Many ordinary people would tend to agree with this – even if they take it no further than ensuring they answer the telephone with their left ear when discussing business, while reserving their right ear for affairs of the heart. There is of course some truth in it all, overlaid with a thick layer of superstition and wishful thinking. For while it is generally true that the two sides of the brain control different activities, it is also true that in people who suffer brain damage the unimpaired hemisphere can take over functions normally performed by the other side. So it is debatable whether our 'metaphysical amnesia' (if indeed we suffer from it) is physiologically related to the structure of our brains. We also cannot escape the fact that, though New Agers complain about the one-sided thinking that western culture promotes, their own understanding of consciousness is itself ultimately reductionist and rationalist. It is inconsistent to contend that anything that can be intuitively verified through the right brain is OK, while logical verification through the left brain is somehow suspect. Whatever else it may be, this kind of reasoning is certainly no more holistic than the inadequate system it is supposed to replace. At the same time, the general points that New Agers are making, though exaggerated, can hardly be denied.

In reality, we all know that rational understanding is only half the story. Our everyday relationships with other people tell us that there is more to life than that. A lot more. For in that realm, 'belief' has more to do with personal commitment and open communication than with the mere acceptance of facts. If my belief in my partner consisted only of knowledge of rationally verifiable data such as her birth date, her size, her hair colour and so on, then we would have a very strange understanding of each other. A relationship cannot proceed very far before emotions and feelings come into the picture – even that supremely non-rational feeling we call 'love'.

By contrast, in the mainstream western Christian tradition, 'knowing God' has for the most part meant knowing things about God – quite often pretty abstruse and esoteric things, at that. Belief in God has majored on 'facts' about God rather than direct personal experience of God's presence. It was once said of the nineteenth-century English churchman, Cardinal John Henry Newman, that he believed in God but didn't trust God. Shirley Maclaine puts it even more succinctly in her report of a conversation with 'John', a channeled spirit entity who comments: 'Your religions teach religion – not spirituality.'[2] It is the search for spirituality – a mystical, personal, direct encounter with 'God' – that is at the heart of much of the New Age Movement. And in this quest, it is inevitable that hands-on experience is going to be far more important than mere intellectual belief.

SOME BASIC BELIEFS

Having said all that, when New Agers claim they have no beliefs, they are not quite coming clean. The conviction that subjective experience is more important than objective fact is itself a belief, which may or may not be true. Beyond that, there are also other basic assumptions that look suspiciously like a belief system. In seeking to identify some core to the New Age philosophy, Marilyn Ferguson observes that 'the mystical experience of wholeness encompasses all separation'. What this amounts to is a belief that everything in the universe is one: 'This wholeness encompasses self, others, ideas . . . You are joined to a great Self . . . And because that Self is inclusive, you are joined to all others.'[3] There is a 'life force', 'energy field' or 'consciousness' that animates the whole of existence. It is found in people and animals, but it also runs through every part of the natural world – grass, trees, mountains, stones, stars, galaxies and much more besides. They are all bound together into one great system by this energy field that is common to them all. In fact, it is the only ultimate reality there is. This means that finding true meaning and fulfilment in life is a matter of recognizing and accepting one's place in this great cosmic scheme of things.

This point of view is more widely held in the west today than most people realize. The average person in the street may not express it in this kind of jargon. But I well remember that when *Star Wars* (the first of a long series of Hollywood blockbusters based on the discovery of spiritual forces) was released, conventional greetings like 'Good morning' or 'Good afternoon' were replaced almost overnight by cosmic statements such as 'May the Force be with you.' Other box office successes have been dominated by similar themes. Indiana Jones gains his reputation by searching for all sorts of magical and spiritual keys to the meaning of life and the cosmos, while films like *ET* and *Gremlins* affirm the reality of some extraterrestrial life force – and the *Superman* series depicts a hero from another world not only entering our own, but through his superior power and ancient wisdom actually putting right many of the wrongs and injustices that concern us all so deeply.

Film critics have had a field day trying to discern and analyze the religious messages coming from modern Hollywood. *ET*, for example, has been compared with the story of Jesus in the Christian Bible. Al Millar, an American professor of biblical literature, wrote a pamphlet called *ET – You're more than a movie star*, in which he noted over thirty parallels between ET's visitation and that of the Christian saviour Jesus. Others have seen more sinister messages lurking behind such films, while director Steven Spielberg denies there is any religion in his films at all! Whether religious themes are incorporated deliberately is debatable, but there can be little doubt that certain spiritual assumptions lie at the back of all these productions. In particular, there is the idea that the term 'God' means the cosmic process rather than the personal and powerful being of the old Judaeo-Christian worldview. Contrasting the old 'Machine Age God' of the Age of Pisces with the new 'Systems Age God' of the Age of Aquarius, internationally acclaimed management consultant Russell Ackoff encapsulates the essence of this contemporary view when he says that the New Age 'God' 'cannot be individualized or personified, and cannot be thought of as the creator . . . In this holistic view of things man is taken as a part of God just as his heart is taken as a part of man'.[4] Transpersonal psychologist Scott Peck says pretty much the same thing: 'If you desire wisdom greater than your own, you can find it inside you . . . To put it plainly, our unconscious is God . . . It is for the individual to become totally, wholly God.'[5]

RELIGIOUS ROOTS

This view has some interesting antecedents in the world of traditional religion. Anyone who is familiar with the religious thought of India will recognize here certain similarities with classical Hinduism. The idea that ultimate reality ('God', if you like) consists of a kind of cosmic essence which is present in all things is very similar to the concept of Brahman, the universal Reality which was prior to all other existence. And the insistence on personal experience as a thing of greater authority than holy books or theological 'beliefs' also has its parallel in the *Gita*, which states, 'As is a pool of water in a place flooded with water, so are all the Vedas [traditional Hindu scriptures] to a person who has attained Enlightenment.'[6]

But it comes as no surprise to discover that New Age thinking at this point is not quite the same as Hinduism. New Agers tend to take something that appeals to them, and modify it by combination with other things that also appeal to them. In this case, parts of a Hindu worldview rub shoulders with bits of western culture in ways that both traditional Hindus and western Christians would think strange. For in the east, Atman (the individual self) *is* Brahman. As soon as you say that, individual people lose their distinctive identity – something that has little appeal for the western 'me generation' which has largely produced the New Age. But in a system that has no place for logical thinking and is organized purely on the basis of what is useful – what feels right – that is no problem. You can simply combine western individualism with eastern mysticism, and give it a new twist. 'Sure, all things are divine – especially me!!' As someone put it to me: 'The drop never goes into the bucket – the whole bucket gets absorbed into the drop.'

Related to this is the fact that whereas Hinduism is essentially world-denying, seeing salvation in terms of escape from attachment to this material world, New Age people tend to be world-affirming. They don't want to reject the world – they would rather enjoy it and change it. So you can have the best of everything. It is possible both to have your cake and eat it, after all! In fact, cynics would go further. For this kind of religious mixture

enables you to depersonalize evil, while still keeping
people in the centre of things. The New Ager has an open
door to personal fulfilment in this world, without having
to accept personal responsibility either here or anywhere
else. Some New Agers – by no means all – resist this kind
of innuendo. They usually do this by arguing that since all
religions contain some truth – however obscured and
hidden it may be – then the 'wisdom of the ages' will
be discerned by combining insights from different
traditions. Since organized religion has historically been
the cause of some of the world's fiercest conflicts, such a
move towards harmonization might actually speed up the
dawning of that age of peace and mutual acceptance that
we all long for.

LOOKING FOR ANSWERS

This explains why many New Agers are content to take
elements from all over the spiritual and metaphysical
spectrum in what can seem an indiscriminate and, at
times, incoherent way. If we start from the basic
assumption that 'all is one', then it naturally follows that
life can find its deepest meaning as people get in tune
with this one great cosmic life force. But what is it that
separates us from it anyway? A common answer is that
separation from the divine force of the cosmos is the
creation only of our own consciousness. In that case, we
can be 'saved' by utilizing techniques that will lead to the
realignment of consciousness. Instead of remaining on
the purely rational (left-brained) level, where our culture
has conditioned and trained us to operate, we can move
on to the attainment of a higher level of consciousness – a
(right-brained) spiritual and metaphysical level. By doing
this we will get to the bottom of things, find our own inner

self and, ultimately, undergo personal transformation. Inevitably, different people will feel a need for change and self-discovery at different points in their experience. Which helps to explain the bewildering assortment of transformational practices that can all, to one degree or another, be identified as 'New Age' – ranging from demanding physical exercises and tough challenge to alternative medicine and more traditional spiritual activities, and ultimately shading off into areas dominated by the occult.

Some of the techniques currently in vogue are mind-blowing, both in their overall variety and in their individual character. Your personal starting-point might, for instance, be an awareness of irrational and uncontrollable fears and phobias. If so, you might like to take some advice from Angie Stephenson. Originally from Wetherby, a sleepy country town in rural Yorkshire, she now specializes in helping people to discover themselves by walking over burning coals at 1,300 degrees centigrade! First introduced to the idea herself while leading self-awareness workshops, she comments: 'I knew fire-walking was another experience for opening and expanding people. But it's a risky business . . . I think people are hungry to find out more meaning in their lives. It came as a big surprise to me to know I could walk on fire. Intellectually, I knew all about positive thinking, but walking on hot coals has given me direct experience. It's taken a big chunk of my timidity away.'

To walk on fire under expert guidance requires not only courage and time, but cash. A typical session can cost at least £80 sterling. So why not take some advice from San Francisco accountant Irving William Bernstein, who combines spiritual counsel with adroit investment of your funds. 'After 22 years as a certified public accountant,' he says, 'I discovered that being a whole person includes financial maturity as well as personal growth. I reached a nurturing balance in my own life, and now through the blending of Financial Principles with Transformational work, I am able to support people's financial well-being in a unique way.' He's not the only one, of course. For years traditional tele-evangelists like Robert Schuller have been offering almost the same thing, while there is no shortage of Christians in the mainline churches who will tell you that faithfulness to God as they define it will also bring a financial reward.

But maybe money isn't your problem. Perhaps it's your physical appearance that is preventing you from discovering your real self. In that case, why not have a personal colour consultation? 'Learn to use your colors for healing, self-confidence and balance in your life,' says the Looksmart programme, explaining that 'color is electro-magnetic energy and each color has a certain vibration or frequency that is beneficial to your good health.' The pursuit of physical health through one means or another is widely perceived as a key with which one may unlock the personal psyche. The Reichian bioenergetic bodywork system is a comprehensive method for coming to grips with one's spiritual self. This was devised by psychologist Wilhelm Reich (1897–1957), who began as a follower of Sigmund Freud, but soon developed his own theory that there was a close relationship between the body's muscle patterns and psychological well-being. He believed that the 'character armour' constructed by the muscles needed to be realigned by exposure to the 'orgone energy' which ran through the whole universe. He developed a complex system of 'bodywork' which, he claimed, brought about this realignment. Peter Bernhardt is a contemporary practitioner of this therapy who, having trained in London, has practised all over the world. He says it includes 'breathing awareness, centering, grounding, boundary exercises, emotional release work, and imagery'. Many testify that it has led them into higher levels of consciousness and renewed spiritual understanding. This is but one of a large number of similar methods – all of them based on controlled breathing and many of them including the use of evocative New Age music – which are claimed to have the power to expand consciousness and lead their practitioners into a deeper exploration of their inner selves.

Other more physically demanding techniques are also widely used to produce an enhanced spiritual openness. Sky-diving may not be to everyone's taste, but there are some slightly less threatening therapies available. The martial arts are claimed to be especially beneficial in this respect, and are certainly more than just a form of physical exercise. One practitioner of Tai Chi described it to me as 'a lifestyle which promotes natural self-discipline, respect and enfoldment. The practice of the art daily – preferably among trees and birds and flowers and plenty of fresh air – will fill one's days with purpose and joy that only comes when the soul is reintegrated with nature.' In their book *The Psychic Side of Sports*, Michael Murphy and Rhea A. White claim that any physical activity can enhance spiritual awareness: 'The many reports we have collected show us that sport has enormous power to sweep us beyond the ordinary sense of self to evoke capacities that have generally been regarded as mystical, occult, or religious.'[7] In other words, when your favourite soccer star scores a goal and then runs up and down the pitch in ecstasy, hugging his team-mates, he may not be just deliriously happy – he could also be in an altered state of consciousness, or having an out-of-body experience, or going through some other form of heightened spiritual awareness!

Getting in touch with nature – or, rather, with the spiritual powers of Gaia, mother earth – is also the aim behind the many wilderness quests on which New Agers embark in search of personal meaning and transformation. In the course of her well-publicized spiritual search, Shirley Maclaine visited the Peruvian Andes, and the mountains played a particular role in her remarkable self-discovery. Not everyone can make it to South America. But for those who are not quite so well off, Mount Shasta in California provides a comparable environment in a place which is said to be specially close to the spiritual powers of the universe. The same beneficial effects are sometimes claimed for treks into the Aboriginal homelands of the Australian outback. Some operators even offer package tours to 'the power centres of the earth' – places where spiritual searchers can not only find personal healing as they align themselves with the mother goddess, but can also contribute towards the healing of the earth itself, which has been scarred and impaired by generations of insensitive technological exploitation. In the UK, major stopping places on such an itinerary would include Stonehenge and Glastonbury in England, and Findhorn and Iona in Scotland.

Yoga and other body exercises are also popular methods of self-discovery. The 'Dances of Universal Peace', for example, were first evolved in the United States in 1967 by Samuel Lewis, under the guidance of his own teachers, Ruth St Denis and Sufi Inayat Khan. But they have now spread around the world and are presently taught in at least fourteen countries. Their stated aim is quite simple: 'The Dances of Universal Peace are an art of movement and sound with feeling that can allow one to move in a new way, to feel unity within and without. The energy created in the circle can fuel life and work on many levels.' One does not need to be a dancer in order to take part – one needs 'only a desire to move with devotion and rhythm, dedicating oneself to experiencing joy and peace for the benefit of all beings'. A concept that is taken a stage further by groups like the Sun Dancers of San Rafael, California, who describe themselves as a dance company which 'celebrates the magical force and wonder of the female and dedicates its artistic and teaching endeavours to the dignity and empowerment of all life and to the preservation of Mother Earth'. Simpler exercises for the same purpose are offered by dance teacher Barbara Bye, who leads informal groups of spiritual searchers through the nature parks of northern California every Tuesday morning. The object of these treks is 'to do movement and exercises and attune the body with the Earth, the environment and the basic elements'.

For those with a more mystical bent, something like Rebirthing might be appealing. Essentially a series of breathing exercises, this is another widely used technique for getting in touch with one's inner self. Bob Frissell, who describes himself as 'a certified rebirther of ten years', says it is 'a course designed to help you resolve issues on your true work, money and authority figures, while aligning with universal principles . . . Rebirthing is the process of getting to know and love your Self. It has to do with freeing your breath, choosing your thoughts, expressing your feelings and healing your body. In essence, it is spiritual purification.' An experience that in turn can lead to renewed clarity on a whole range of topics, including health, relationships and sexuality, as well as more esoteric spiritual dimensions. Karen Hughes, hypnotherapist and channeler from West Goshen, Pennsylvania, describes the benefits of such activities: 'I did the fire walk with Tony Robbins. I did metal-bending . . . I've had an out-of-body experience. I hear voices and I see things . . . it has all led me to a different position, which is very, very grounded.'

Those heading for overtly spiritual experiences are more likely to look to channeling and past-life therapies as a means of expanding their consciousness and gaining personal transformation and enlightenment. These are the techniques that tend to grab the headlines whenever the New Age is being discussed – and they are certainly spectacular. But some claim that it is also possible for such experiences to be produced by purely technological methods. In the last two or three years the market has been flooded by a bewildering array of so-called electronic mind machines. The inventors of these devices claim that by a mixture of visual and aural stimuli they can induce subtle changes in brainwave patterns leading to altered states of consciousness that can enhance creativity, influence moods, impart greater powers of concentration, speed up learning processes, make you stronger and fitter, and give you a super-charged sex life. Mind gymnasiums, a fashionable form of relaxation for Japanese executives in the seventies, can now be found in the leafy suburbs of several English towns and cities. And if you know where to go, you can even buy a portable device the size of a Walkman that will induce altered states as you walk along the street.

DIMENSIONS OF CONSCIOUSNESS

So what exactly is consciousness? And what do people mean when they talk of moving from one dimension of consciousness to another? To put it simply, there are two kinds of people: ordinary mortals, and transformed or enlightened ones. To be ordinary is to have a mind that is not aware of itself. To be transformed is to be aware of your mind, conscious of your own consciousness. By moving into the 'fourth dimension' of consciousness, a person is empowered to see the other three dimensions in a new way. And every other dimension beyond the fourth brings a further enhancement in self-knowledge. In the words of Marilyn Ferguson, 'The fourth dimension is not another place; it is *this* place, and it is immanent in us, a process.'[8] It is commonly claimed that we do not automatically enjoy this enhanced consciousness because the two hemispheres of our brains have somehow drifted apart. Our lives are dominated and controlled by left-brained functions – things that major on the rational. Whereas the possibility of inner knowing and spiritual transformation is locked away in the right brain. To put it simply, the right brain corresponds to the 'heart', while the left brain is the 'mind'.

Within ourselves, therefore, we are a microcosm of the society we have created. Just as there is division and fragmentation all around us, so we are inwardly fragmented and broken. The two aspects of our personality do not know how to communicate with one another. As a result, we live generally disjointed and unsatisfactory lives. In order to evolve a more holistic internal existence, we need to remove the blockages that prevent the rational self from interacting with and being directed by the spiritual self. A transformed consciousness is one in which this integration has been achieved. Therapists sometimes speak of healing 'the wounded child' within us. This can be, quite literally, wounded fragments of childhood experience that have a damaging effect on adult personalities. But the term can also mean your 'Higher Self', an aspect of personality that features a lot in discussions about channeling. In the words of Reenie Davison, a psychologist working with US military personnel,

> The Inner Child is the spirit within us that underlies all our life experience ... When the child is feeling free and healthy, we approach life with confidence and enthusiasm. However, if we have experienced trauma, abandonment, or lack of sufficient love and nurturing ... the child is wounded. We become, on some level, dysfunctional ... Together we will develop a system that will enable you to participate fully in healing past emotional wounds, as well as restructuring current attitudes and negative beliefs about Self.

Since we are complex beings, with body and mind continually interacting with each other, reorganizing one aspect of ourselves can also facilitate and enhance the restructuring and realignment or our whole being. This is where the various techniques for self-realization come into the picture. For when we interfere with any single part of our whole being, that interrupts the old, familiar, compartmentalized way in which we all live, and opens us up to new dimensions of experience and understanding. Such interference can begin anywhere, which is why energetic sports like skiing or scuba-diving can rub shoulders with bodywork exercises like Rolfing or rebirthing as consciousness-enhancing techniques. But once the mechanistic cycle has been broken, things will never be the same again. Self-awareness leads to the discovery of yet other dimensions of consciousness – transpersonal, cosmic, global and universal. The individual self becomes aware of being part of a collective social self – and beyond that, of the transcendent universal Self that is the ground of all things.

There can be no doubt that those who use these techniques as an entry into expanded consciousness, spiritual awareness, personal discovery and transformation are seriously searching for meaning in life. They are looking within themselves because, in a world stripped of its traditional sources of authority and spiritual guidance, there is nowhere else to look. In that sense, much of what is going on can be labelled self-centred. It can also be deceptive and, ultimately, destructive.

We need not question the claim that it is possible to enter into altered states of consciousness by such methods. But when these things are treated as ends in themselves, serious New Agers begin to feel distinctly unhappy about it all. One New Age therapist told me with concern, 'These phenomena are all real, but they're being taken out of context. It's the seduction of thinking they're "it" that makes people go off the path. In order to understand the phenomena properly people need to be grounded in a deeper tradition.' The superficial approach is a bit like seeing Jesus only as a wonder-worker, without also taking account of the broader implications of his total teaching.

SERIOUS SEARCHERS

This is why a significant number of New Age people would disparage what they regard as the simplistic view that is prepared to utilize all kinds of diverse techniques without regard to their origins and background. One such serious searcher put it to me quite plainly: 'One of the things that strikes me about a lot of the people who call themselves "New Age" is that they take a little bit from a lot of different traditions, and haven't put all the bits together in a coherent perception of the universe. I think that is a real danger, because you can avoid a lot of difficult questions by taking a little bit from here and there.' By contrast, the serious searchers tend to concentrate on one particular spiritual path. It may be some kind of oriental philosophy, such as Zen or Taoism, or some aspect of ancient western paganism. But for many, it will be something that has links with the mainstream western Christian tradition. For it is widely believed that Jesus too was a great 'spiritual master', whose teachings originally reflected the radical, practical spirituality of the East – but all that was lost with his adoption as a western hero and the absorption of his message into the western cultural matrix.

You don't have to look far into Christian history to find some possible New Age options. One of the most popular is Gnosticism. This was an ancient heterodox form of Christianity, dating back to the second century AD, which laid great emphasis on precisely those things that many people find absent from the modern western Church. Not only did it centre on various mystical rituals and spiritual experiences, but it also reversed traditional gender roles – women could be, and frequently were, Gnostic priests. Its worldview, though different from the Hindu outlook, insisted that there was a divine spark or life-force running through much of human experience. Just to add to its attractions, it had its own secret 'gospels' which claimed to reveal the 'true' picture of Jesus. The Gnostic Jesus, who is very different to the Jesus of the Bible, turns out to be a revealer of spiritual secrets who would feel totally at home in modern California!

Back in the 1970s, I spent several years researching ancient Gnosticism for a PhD degree at the University of Manchester, England. At that time, I never dreamed it would equip me so well for understanding the modern New Age Movement. I certainly could not have imagined that the ancient Gnostic texts which had been found buried in a heap of bird manure at Nag Hammadi in Upper Egypt, where they had been abandoned centuries before, would be seized upon so eagerly and would become sacred documents again to space-age spiritual travellers. I shared all this with a New Age psychologist in northern California, by way of introducing myself to him. I shall never forget his response: 'Gnosticism? I felt my whole body smile at that word.'

He was one of the many thousands who have made themselves familiar with Gnostic texts like *The Gospel of Thomas*, *The Gospel of Philip*, *The Gospel of Truth* and others found at Nag Hammadi. They were all originally written in Coptic – a hybrid language related to Egyptian hieroglyphics and ancient Greek – so there are not too many people around who can read it today! But the worldview of these texts is very congenial to New Agers. Thomas' Jesus makes metaphysical pronouncements that could have come straight out of a modern handbook on self-discovery. Like this typical example: 'It is I who am the light which is above them all. It is I who am the All. From Me did the All come forth, and unto Me did the All extend.'[9] The texts were discovered towards the end of the Second World War, and the first ones began to appear in English translations in the 1950s. The only people who were really interested at the time were scholars of religion, and various crooked antique dealers who made a fortune by circulating the originals on the black market in Europe and the Middle East. The way in which *The Gospel of Thomas* was first published – with the Coptic text printed on one page, and an English translation on the page facing – only served to emphasize its essentially scholarly appeal. It was put out in Holland by E. J. Brill of Leiden, a specialist press whose reputation was founded on the high-class production of short-run books for the academic market. I don't know how many copies of *The Gospel of Thomas* were sold in Europe, but I imagine that most of the books on Brill's lists are doing pretty well if they make the 1,000 mark. Yet when the same Coptic translation hit the US market under the imprint of an American publisher, things were decidedly different, and this slim volume sold nearly 100,000 copies! In due course, the entire Nag Hammadi Gnostic library became available in English translation – and the same thing happened. Almost 50,000 copies of a hardback edition went overnight, followed by another 80,000 in a paperback version. A new revised edition has recently come from the presses, and the phenomenon is repeating itself.

ANCIENT PATHS FOR MODERN PILGRIMS

For an intriguing glimpse into the fascination of this particular spiritual path, come with me to the California town of Palo Alto. At first glance, it looks much like any other bedroom suburb, until you realize that this is the centre of Silicon Valley, and also home to prestigious Stanford University. The old and the new live together here quite happily. Hi-tech boffins expand the frontiers of technology with ever-increasing speed in impressive buildings of glass and steel, while at the same time others spend their lives delving into the mysteries of the past in the more relaxed atmosphere of Stanford's old Spanish colonial-style campus. But even in the futurist environment of microprocessors, computers and robotics, there is more than a hint of another ancient and more mystical world. For a good number of the factories where silicon chips are carefully crafted into the raw materials of artificial intelligence are intriguingly constructed in the shape of ancient pyramids – a profile which, according to legend, has magical powers to concentrate cosmic and spiritual energy. Here too is one of the largest metaphysical bookstores in northern California – Minerva Books on Alma Street. And Palo Alto is also Gnostic territory. The Ecclesia Gnostica Mysteriorum, just a little further along Alma Street, offers to balance the quest for technological advance with an inner search for spiritual self-knowledge.

The publicity handout sounds suitably cryptic and compelling: 'We teach the individual to reach the state in which gnosis can be made manifest . . . through the understanding of the rich legacy of early myths and symbolism from numerous sources . . . and through ritual, celebrating . . . archetypical acts of ceremonial communion with the timeless realities of the soul.' After that, it comes as something of an anticlimax to discover that all this takes place in a small neighbourhood shopping centre, where the Gnostic church nestles in a first-floor suite between real estate and lawyers' offices on the one side, and a Lucky's supermarket on the other. Or maybe this is an appropriate location for a religion whose very existence is clothed in mystery and depends on the belief that there is more to life than meets the eye.

Once inside the Gnostic Center, things begin to look

rather different. The stairs up to the first floor can hardly
be described as anything other than functional. But they
lead into a light and airy room with stained glass windows,
accommodating perhaps fifty or sixty people seated in
chairs. At one end, in striking contrast with the rest of the
building, stands an elaborate altar. Here the drab
functional lines give way to mystical symbols of many
kinds, and as the Gnostic eucharist gets under way there
is all the buzz and excitement of an ancient mystery being
lovingly re-created to speak again to the human needs of
our modern world. The altar, standing two steps higher
than the main floor level, is bathed in light, much of it
emanating from the many candles placed all around, and
attractively decorated with flowers and peacock feathers.
There is a simple bronze figurine in the centre of the end
wall.

   The worshippers are a typical cross-section of modern
society, all united by the fact that they find that this
particular ritual helps them to discover themselves. It
reveals to them, in the words of one ancient Gnostic text,
'the knowledge of who we were, and what we have
become, where we were or where we were placed,
whither we hasten, from what we are redeemed, what
birth is, and what rebirth.' Many such texts are used in
the course of the service, but modern hymns and prayers
also play a part. In fact, the Gnostic eucharist itself turns
out to be remarkably similar to a traditional Christian
Mass in the Roman Catholic tradition. The presiding
(female) bishop is dressed in a simple white gown, with an
attractive stole colourfully decorated with floral patterns.
Other priests, both male and female, also take part in the
ritual, wearing surplices vaguely reminiscent of Christian
vestments, though there is more than a hint of the
classical Roman toga about them. There are incense,

wafers and a large goblet of wine. And as the ceremony proceeds, there is singing – mostly harmonic chanting, a musical hybrid somewhere between traditional Gregorian chants and the contemporary music of the French ecumenical Taizé community – together with readings and prayers. Four male priests hold a canopy over the altar, not unlike the *huppa* at a Jewish wedding, while the women priests and the wine of the eucharist are conspicuously veiled.

'The veils on the women and the veil on the wine symbolize the same thing as the transformation of the bread and wine. It is a veil in which the divinity, the presence of the extraordinary – Christ, God, whatever you want to call it – hides.' That is how Rosamonde Miller, the bishop of this Gnostic church, explains what is going on. She was born in Languedoc, the home of the thirteenth-century French Gnostic sect known as the Cathars. At the age of nineteen she had a remarkable religious experience in a Cuban prison cell, and later joined the French mystical Order of Mary Magdalene. She has been the leader of the Palo Alto Gnostics since 1978. Her philosophy is simple: 'Our church has no dogmas and no beliefs. Beliefs hinder the experience of Gnosis.' True to this ideal, you don't have to be a member or undergo any special ceremony such as baptism in order to belong. You don't even have to be a Gnostic! Communion is offered to all comers at 10.30 on Sunday mornings. As the publicity handout says: 'No barrier is erected around the altar of the Gnosis.'

The Gnostic church is not an organization. Bishop Miller knows of twelve other similar groups around the world, but her congregation has no formal ties with them. Not all of them actually use the name 'Gnostic'. The Liberal Catholic Church, for example, is essentially a

Gnostic group with branches in the UK, Australia and other countries (though, surprisingly, it finds a place in *The UK Christian Handbook* as a mainline Christian church). There is obviously enormous interest in the subject, and when Jay Kinney founded the glossy *Gnosis* magazine in the late 1980s, it had no trouble establishing a circulation of more than 10,000 within little more than three years.

What is distinctive about the Gnostic way of understanding things? According to the ancient Gnostic myths, this world is not the only one, nor is it the most important for those who want to find the real meaning of life. There are in fact two worlds – this one, dominated by materialism and corruption, and another more spiritual world where 'God' is and where true fulfilment and enlightenment may be found. The ancient Gnostics told many stories to explain how this enlightenment could be achieved, usually understanding it within a framework of what today would be called reincarnation. The chance to escape from the bondage of material existence comes at death, they suggested, when it is possible for the human soul to reach the world of spirit. The problem is, not everyone is spiritually equipped to make the transition. To do so, a person needs to have a divine 'spark' embedded in their nature – otherwise they will return to the world to start another meaningless round of humdrum existence. And even those who have the 'spark' cannot be certain of getting out, unless they have been enlightened about their own nature. For this to happen, 'knowledge' (*gnosis* in Greek – hence the name) is required. Not intellectual, rational knowledge, but a personal 'knowing' of oneself and, ultimately, of the spiritual ground of the cosmos.

Modern Gnostics do not always articulate all this in the same mythological framework used by their ancient predecessors. Nor do they treat their ancient scriptures as a source for theology and dogma. Instead, Gnostic ideas from the past become symbols by which to explain some of modern life's mysteries. Viewed in that light, the message is a simple New Age analysis. We are all outsiders in a meaningless world, trapped in systems and societies which create division and disharmony among people and, ultimately, prevent us from relating to the spiritual side of existence, through which alone we can discover true meaning and satisfaction. And how is such meaning to be discovered? By ignoring the false images of the world as we know it, and finding the common identity between our own innermost self and the ultimate spiritual power of the cosmos.

This angle on life makes sense for many people. It formed a basis for much of the psychology of C. G. Jung. Also, it bears more than a passing resemblance to modern western existentialist philosophy. It also provides an answer to the age-old problem of pain and suffering. Who is responsible for a world where things have gone so badly wrong? If God made all things, did God make evil as well? The traditional Christian answer is that God made things good, and people messed them up. But the Gnostic simply accepts pain and suffering as an unavoidable tragedy that is an integral part of life itself. It is not God's fault. Nor is it our fault. In fact, the true God is as much an alien in this world as we are. From the vantage point of Gnostic spirituality, the world itself is an illusion, and only rekindled spiritual vision can give it reality and meaning. That is why true knowledge is not a matter of knowing theology or of holding to certain beliefs, but of knowing oneself.

Lance Beizer is an attorney and also the presiding bishop of the Ecclesia Gnostica Sacramentorum in San Jose, California. 'When I found the Gnostic church,' he explains, 'it resonated well within me as a church which provided me with the ritual, the contact with God, the way through the eucharist service to my soul, without binding me into any kind of demand that I adhere to a particular doctrinal position.' Rosamonde Miller explains a bit more: 'Gnosis is a knowledge of the heart. It is not a knowledge that can be imposed. We all have the equipment and the capability for it, but we have been deprived of the ability to recognize the spiritual frame of reference, which is constantly within and around us.'

The problem is that we are ignorant of ourselves, and to achieve salvation and wholeness we need to break through this ignorance and into full spiritual consciousness. The ritual of the Gnostic eucharist is one way to do this. Though the externals of bread and wine are the same as those used in mainline Christian churches, the theology is different. And so is the experience. Instead of being a celebration and a commemoration of an event that happened 2,000 years ago, the Gnostic eucharist has a timeless quality about it. As one worshipper put it to me, 'It's an experience that's happening right now and in this place, and we're living it.'

In addition to the private, internal experiences that the worshippers have as they go within themselves in this way, the symbolism also conveys an image of a new age of harmony and peace. Most obviously, perhaps, in the way women play a full and equal role with men – not only in the ritual, but in all the images and metaphors used to describe the ultimate spiritual reality of God. The balance of the masculine and feminine principles as a way of getting the cosmos right is an important part of Gnostic thinking, just as it has also played a part in alchemy, in Taoism, in Hinduism, in various modern psychological theories and in holistic medicine. Indeed, some of the ancient Gnostic texts have a woman – Mary Magdalene – among the apostles of Christ. Psychoanalyst June Singer, a regular worshipper with the Palo Alto Gnostics, finds this one of Gnosticism's most appealing features: 'I found something I had been wanting for a long time in a religion – a place where I could feel as a woman an active equal participant, not only in the service itself but in the philosophy behind the service.'

Feeling a bit clueless? Well, that is probably par for the course. For the experience of self-discovery is not one that can easily be communicated from one person to another. Indeed, if it could be, then it might not be the real thing. As Lance Beizer put it: 'As a Gnostic priest, I operate as an intermediary rather than a teacher. You can teach a foreign language, or that Jesus was born at a particular time and died at a certain time, and that his death has a certain kind of meaning. But that sort of information is not the same as knowledge of what religion is, what God is, what our own society is. That is not a thing that can either be taught, or even communicated. The central idea of Gnosticism is the *gnosis kardias*, or knowledge of the heart. That is unrelated to intellectual activity: it has to do with the individual ability to perceive truth. Down at bottom, we have to make our own determinations and decisions. A gnosis that can be taught just isn't the true gnosis.' Rosamonde Miller says simply, 'In the Gnostic tradition, you don't follow what has been written. You follow what is found experientially – within yourself.' The connexions between this and the search for spirituality through psychological self-exploration are obvious. It is not surprising that when Carl Jung was asked if he believed in God, he replied in typically Gnostic fashion, 'I know: I don't need to believe.'

To follow a single specific pathway in the search for

personal enlightenment and self-knowledge is obviously a very demanding thing. To make progress calls for discipline and hard work, not to mention an esoteric mind-set that does not come easily to many western people. This probably explains why most New Agers prefer to experiment with a whole variety of techniques for spiritual fulfilment, rather than sticking with just one possibility. And in any case, there are so many ways to 'go within' that different people are likely to have their own favourite methods. Even one individual, with changing moods and experiences, may well find that different things appeal at different periods of his or her life. In this spiritual search, the important thing is to do what feels right just now. At some other time something completely different may well feel right.

Whatever the purists of the New Age Movement may wish, it is impossible to deny that at the present time there are relatively few people who are prepared to stick with a particular spiritual path for too long. In a culture which has encouraged us to expect that anything can be produced almost instantaneously – from coffee to global communications – it is not surprising that instant spirituality also has a tremendous appeal. Especially if that spirituality has every appearance of coming in from some world other than the one we normally experience through our bodily senses. Extraterrestrials, spirit guides, near-death experiences, astral projection, past-life recall – it all sounds like something unreal out of a science fiction thriller. But this is where much of the interest in the New Age Movement is focused today. It is also where a lot of money is being made. And this is the territory into which we head in our next chapter.

Chapter 4

SEARCHING FOR THE UNKNOWN

*F*ROM the very beginning of time, people have been fascinated by the possibility that there may be more to life than the things we can touch, see, and handle. Could there be some other world out there which, though apparently intangible, yet has an extensive and powerful influence on what goes on in the world as we all know it? Throughout recorded history, the overwhelming majority of the world's people have answered that question with a resounding 'Yes!' Some have developed very specific ideas about what happens in such a world. Medieval European artists often painted lurid pictures of both the pains and the pleasures of life in the next world. Others think of another world in a more diffuse way, as a vaguely spiritual or metaphysical sphere of existence. From time to time, belief in other worlds has been both questioned and denied. Indeed, the basic assumption of modern western culture, stemming from the European Enlightenment, has been that there can be no other world than the one we live in every day. Twenty years ago, that was still the dominant opinion among westerners, and those who thought otherwise would have been regarded as cranks or even cases for psychological help. But all that is changing. And it is changing very fast indeed. At the vanguard of this change is the New Age technique of channeling.

TUNING IN TO SPIRIT GUIDES

You might think that with the dominant New Age emphasis on 'going within' to find life's ultimate answers, the last place anyone would turn to would be an old fashioned and seemingly discredited belief in the supernatural in its most bizarre form. But not so! Beings in other dimensions form an important and increasingly popular strand in the colourful tapestry that is today's spiritual search. J. Z. Knight's channeled entity Ramtha is only one of many thousands of disembodied entities being contacted every day in the desperate scramble to make sense out of the jumble that is modern life. For New Agers seeking life-changing messages from other dimensions of consciousness, there are more channels available than there are on a satellite dish. Channelers claim to be receiving cosmic wisdom from a bewildering array of entities. In this expansive spiritual world, dolphins and fairies rub shoulders with beings from the past, extraterrestrials from other planets – and even beings from the future. Spirits currently being channeled include the rich and famous as well as the unknown and esoteric. If you know where to go, channelers claim to be able to put you in contact with celebrities from the past as varied as John Lennon, John the Apostle, Rembrandt and Abraham Lincoln. Some entities even dictate books. *The Course in Miracles* is one of the largest and most popular of today's channeled books. First published in 1975 in three volumes, it contains almost 700 pages of basic text, accompanied by a student handbook and a teacher's manual. It was received in a trance by New York psychologist Helen Schucman between 1965 and 1972, and is alleged to contain messages from, among others, no less a figure than Jesus Christ. Other channeled books are less well known, but no less popular – like the material from an entity called Seth, first received back in the sixties and seventies by Jane Roberts but subsequently received by many other channelers as well.

Whenever a new entity goes into print, publishers rub their hands with glee, for there is no shortage of purchasers. Some have even hit the bestseller lists! The fact that this sort of thing is so popular is clear evidence of many people's deep disillusionment with merely human opinions on the crises now facing the human race. In his book *Conscious Evolution*, transpersonal psychologist Barry McWaters sums it all up like this: 'We are listening for messages of guidance from every possible source; tuning in our astro-radios, talking to dolphins, and listening more and more attentively to the words of those among us with psychic abilities. Is there help out there? Is there guidance in here? Will anyone respond?'[1] A message received by Shirley Maclaine from a disembodied entity called 'John' explains the status of such extraterrestrial guides: 'they are operating . . . on a higher level of awareness and a higher level of technology also. But they are not to be revered as Godlike. They are merely teachers . . . They appear when they are most needed. They serve as a symbol of hope and higher understanding.'[2]

What are these spiritual entities allegedly saying to us? Despite the extraordinary diversity of such spirit guides, their communications are surprisingly stereotyped. They typically speak in somewhat archaic language (frequently English), with a stilted and hesitating form of delivery that demands considerable concentration on the part of their hearers. The messages being delivered also have an amazing similarity, usually assuring humans that this world in which we now exist is not the only one.

In fact, it is not the highest order of reality at all, and existing as we all now do on 'the physical plane' is actually a very limited form of experience. We are all part and parcel of a much larger metaphysical and spiritual world. Insofar as there is a supreme being, you yourself are 'God'. In essence, we are all spiritual beings – only, in contrast to other such beings, we happen to be in bodies just now. We are a part of the absolutely Infinite, which means we have no limitations apart from those we create. That means we choose to be who we now are. The rhetoric is similar to that of the Human Potential Movement, only taken to more radical conclusions. For we will also continue to choose other existences in the future. This present life is only a tiny part of the much larger ongoing cycle of spiritual experience in which we are all engaged. The life we live now is not necessarily the only life we ever have lived – or are ever likely to live. Rebecca Pratt, owner of a crystal store in Chester County, Pennsylvania, channels an entity called Dameon, and sums up his message in a few well-chosen words: 'The entire universe is God. We are part of that God energy. Because of that, we create our own reality.'

How does it all work, then? Most channeled messages reveal that souls exist at different levels of cosmic wisdom. There are baby souls, young souls, mature souls, and old souls – the souls in each level have achieved higher and more advanced wisdom than those in previous levels. The individual's soul (or, more properly, the spiritual core of his or her being – sometimes labelled the 'Higher Self') consciously chooses what he or she will be and do at any given point in time. From the timeless perspective of the cosmic world of spirit, you can (and do) choose to be whoever you want to be. And you can stick with it for as long or as short a time as you please. You have absolute power over how any given incarnate life works out – choosing not only the moment of your birth, but also that of your death and those of all events in between. As Henry Ford once said, 'If you think you can, or you think you can't – you're right.'

You might suppose that being on the physical plane in a body would be somewhat restrictive. But, according to the spirit guides, it need not be. Some people do seem to get locked in a 'negative *karma*', whereby they constantly make unhelpful choices for themselves. But it doesn't have to be like that. For each individual soul is an integral part of the great cosmic Soul, which is absolutely infinite. Through this connexion, all the wisdom and energy there has ever been is available to guide and direct ordinary humans in the here and now. We can tune in to these sources, often called the Akashic Records, through channeling. Shirley Maclaine's 'John' explains it this way: 'This stored energy called the Akashic Records is as vast scrolls heaped in vast libraries. You, as an individual, would be thought of as a single scroll within the libraries, or as a single soul within the mind of God.'[3] In one sense, therefore, tuning in to the Akashic Records can also be thought of as tuning in to another dimension of yourself. Typically, this can be done by keeping in constant contact with your own personal 'spirit guides' – entities chosen by your 'Higher Self' before you came into this particular life, to whom you would relate during this experience of incarnate existence. They are a kind of cosmic conscience, available to redirect you towards the fulfilment of your ultimate spiritual goals.

ORIGINS

Those with a sense of history, or a knowledge of religious traditions around the world, will recognize that there is nothing particularly new in all this. People allowing themselves to be 'possessed' by allegedly spiritual forces can be found in many religious traditions. Witch-doctors, shamans and fortune-tellers have been around for a very long time, and in cultural contexts as varied as the world itself. Mediums of one sort or another are commonplace even in western society, quite separately from any influence the New Age Movement might be exerting. However, the New Age phenomenon has some distinctive elements about it – like the word 'channeling' itself. It is used to distinguish what is going on from the practices of old-fashioned mediums. While mediums typically communicate with the dead (who generally retain the characteristics of their past human life-forms), New Agers are aiming to get in tune with some greater cosmic intelligence that may have no direct connexion at all with life as we know it. The entity Bashar, for example, channeled by Darryl Anka, is said to be an extraterrestrial from the planet Essassani. Of course, we can't see it, because this planet is in a different 'vibrational plane' – but Bashar's spaceship once flew over Los Angeles, which is how he first made contact with humans.

People with a modern western 'scientific' worldview might be forgiven for treating all this with a good deal of scepticism. There is, after all, nothing new in people arguing over whether there are extraterrestrials out there. The debate has been going on more or less throughout history. In ancient Greece, Epicurean and Aristotelian philosophers were talking about it long before the time of Jesus. And it soon became a hot issue for the Christian

Church – though most Christian writers of the early centuries rejected the possibility that there could be other rational beings out there. By the thirteenth century, however, even Christians were reopening the matter, as the writings of previously unexplored ancient civilizations became more accessible. But following the discoveries of people like Galileo and Copernicus, the concept lost much of its attraction, and it came to be taken for granted that to be modern and well-informed automatically entailed the rejection of belief in other worlds.

But an increasing number of people now believe there is something in it, including some scientists. In his 1871 presidential address to the British Association for the Advancement of Science, Sir William Thomson (Lord Kelvin) spoke in these terms of the origins of life itself:

> ... because we all confidently believe that there are at present, and have been from time immemorial, many worlds of life besides our own, we must regard it as probable in the highest degree that there are countless seed-bearing meteoric stones moving about through space ... The hypothesis that life originated on this earth through moss-grown fragments from the ruins of another world may seem wild and visionary; all I maintain is that it is not unscientific.

Such a claim was greeted with both amazement and amusement by the scientific community of his day. But Thomson continued to hold this view throughout his life. Indeed, he amalgamated it with a Darwinian view of evolution – which only served to give it additional credibility. So far as we know, Thomson did not speculate on how we might use our extraterrestrial connexions to improve life today. But it is only a short step from this belief to thinking that, if the human race has gone wrong, then a return to our extraterrestrial roots for advice will be the way to get things right again. This assumption lies at the back of many of the products of today's movie industry. Films such as *Superman*, *ET*, *Altered States*, *Always* and *The Day of the Dolphin* all convey that message.

There have also been many from more mainstream religious backgrounds who have reached the same conclusion. The last two centuries have seen a whole range of groups loosely affiliated to the Christian tradition, in which encounters with extraterrestrial guides have played a major role. Baron Emanuel Swedenborg was born in Stockholm in 1688, but settled in London in 1747. There he had many unusual experiences, which he describes quite precisely in the preface to his eight-volume *Arcana Coelestia*, written entirely in Latin between 1749 and 1756. 'It has been granted me now for some years to be constantly and uninterruptedly in company with spirits and angels,' he wrote, 'hearing them speak and in turn speaking with them.' He apparently made correct predictions of some striking earthly events, including a big fire in Stockholm, and his own death – all of it on the basis of information received from his extraterrestrial guides.

Like J. Z. Knight, the Rev. Thomas Lake Harris (1823–1906) began as a Baptist, but following his encounter with Swedenborgian ideas around 1850, he too committed himself to the quest for contact with extraterrestrial entities, and subsequently dictated a channeled book-length poem called *An Epic of the Starry Heaven*. He describes his experiences in these lines:

A new-born language trembled on my tongue,
Whose tones accorded with the singing stars;
A company of spirits, blithe and young
From Jupiter, and Mercury, and Mars,
Drew near and said to me, 'Three days, dear friend,
Thou art our guest; come, wing thy blessed flight
Through the unavailing ocean of sweet light.'

Ellen G. Harmon (1827–1915) was another recipient of such visions. She married James White, another Baptist minister. He was friendly with a man called William Miller, who predicted that Christ would return in either 1843 or 1844. When his return failed to happen, this 'Great Disappointment' was explained by reference to belief in another world. Christ had in fact moved, they claimed, on 22 October 1844, but only in a cosmic dimension, which was why no one saw Him. But in reality, He had entered the most holy region of the heavens, in order to get ready for His second coming to the earth, which would soon begin. In late 1844, influenced by this belief, Ellen White began to have visions – and in due course she met with extraterrestrials. She publicized her experiences through a magazine called *The Present Truth*, and in the edition for August 1849 she gave the following description of what had happened:

The Lord has given me a view of other worlds. Wings were given me, and an angel attended me from the city to a place that was bright and glorious. The grass of the place was living green, and the birds there warbled a sweet song. The inhabitants of the place were of all sizes; they were noble, majestic, and lovely . . . I asked one of them why they were so much more lovely than those on the earth. The reply was, 'We have lived in strict obedience to the commandments of God, and have not fallen by disobedience, like those on the earth' . . . Then I was taken to a world which had seven moons . . . I could not bear the thought of coming back to this dark world again. Then the angel said, 'You must go back, and if you are faithful, you with the 144,000 shall have the privilege of visiting all the worlds . . .'

Ellen G. White became the founder of the Seventh Day Adventist Church.

One of her contemporaries, Joseph Smith, founded the 'Church of Jesus Christ of the Latter Day Saints' (the Mormons). He too had experiences of another world. Born in 1805 on a farm in Sharon, Vermont, he published *The Book of Mormon* in 1830. He claimed that the book had originally been inscribed on golden plates and then hidden near Palmyra in the state of New York. The location of the hiding place was allegedly revealed to him by Moroni, an angelic being from the New World. *The Book of Mormon* itself is not so very different from mainstream Christian books, and certainly does not promote belief in extraterrestrial worlds. But later documents were more influential, notably *The Doctrine and Covenants* (published in 1835, with later additions) and *The Pearl of Great Price* (published in 1851, though collected from earlier magazine articles). Both of these give credence to belief in extraterrestrial intelligences. Parley P. Pratt's 1855 work, *Key to the Science of Theology*, puts it succinctly:

Gods, angels and men, are all of the same species, one race, one great family widely diffused among the planetary systems, as colonies, kingdoms, nations . . . The great distinguishing difference between one portion of this race and another, consists in the varied grades of intelligence and purity, and also in the variety of spheres occupied by each, in a series of progressive being . . .

Many of the popular hymns used by the Latter Day Saints also contain the same themes.

Ellen G. White and Joseph Smith emerged as two of the most influential figures in nineteenth-century American culture and, along with Ralph Waldo Emerson (1803–1882), they have exerted a profound and lasting effect on the religious mindset of their nation. They all believed in the existence of extraterrestrial entities, and in the possibility of ordinary people making contact with them. Unlike the other two, who were more homespun, Emerson had studied at the prestigious Harvard Divinity School and had then had a distinguished career as the minister at the Second Church of Boston (Congregationalist, later to be Unitarian). But, influenced by his discovery of the teachings of the *Bhagavad Gita*, he resigned and took up a second career as a writer and lecturer. In one of his final sermons (entitled 'Astronomy'), delivered on 27 May 1832 but never published until 1938, he put forward the proposition that Selenites, Jovians and Uranians possess 'far more excellent endowments than . . . mankind'.

As a result of the influence of these and similar people, the Great American Dream has always had a transcendental dimension as well as a material one, defining freedom not only in terms of a comfortable lifestyle for all but also as a direct personal access to the realms of the spiritual.

Similar aspirations surfaced in the work of some well-known British writers of the time, particularly in the poetry of Shelley, Wordsworth, Tennyson and the romantic visionary William Blake. In his poem 'Timbuctoo', written in 1829, Tennyson describes how

> *. . . other things talking in unknown tongues,*
> *And notes of busy life in distant worlds*
> *Beat like a far wave on my anxious ear.*

He gives a more personal dimension to these ideas in his 'Ode on the death of the Duke of Wellington', written in 1852 when he was Poet Laureate:

> *For tho the Giant Ages heave the hill*
> *And break the shore, and evermore*
> *Make and break, and work their will,*
> *Tho world on world in myriad myriads roll*
> *Round us, each with different powers,*
> *And other forms of life than ours,*
> *What know we greater than the soul?*

Philip James Bailey (1816–1902) projects a similar cosmology onto Christ himself, who in his poem 'Festus' says:

> *'Think not I lived and died for thine alone,*
> *And that no other sphere hath hailed me Christ.*
> *My life is ever suffering for love.*
> *In judging and redeeming worlds is spent*
> *Mine everlasting being.'*

The debate has never reached a conclusion. Some from within the broad Christian tradition accepted both the existence and the direct guidance of extraterrestrials. Others argued that such beliefs were essentially incompatible with the traditional Christian doctrine of the incarnation of Jesus. As a result, people like the American Transcendentalists abandoned conventional Christianity altogether, while others, because of their Christian convictions, rejected the possibility of other worlds. Contemporary protagonists in the debate divide on broadly the same grounds. Those who reject Christianity often believe in planetary paradises populated by extraterrestrials, who will in due time save us all by direct (and benevolent) intervention. For example, Professor Carl Sagan, a respected American astronomer who has spent much time searching for radio signals beaming in towards us from outer space, suggests that 'it is possible that among the first contents of such a message may be detailed prescriptions for the avoidance of technological disaster'.

MAKING CONNEXIONS

In his article, 'Channeling, a short history of a long tradition', John White suggests that 'it will not be long, fifty years perhaps, before "channeling" will be considered the norm rather than the exception . . . One's "teachers" or "spirit guides" will be as common as one's professors at a university.'[4] For many people, what was once a heresy – both scientific and religious – has now become the prevailing truth of our generation. If it is not actually a religion, then it is certainly some kind of alternative to religion. According to Michael J. Crowe, author of the definitive history of the debate, something like three-fourths of the most influential astronomers of all time, and about half the leading intellectuals of the eighteenth and nineteenth centuries, have at some time entertained the idea of extraterrestrial entities. One of the weaknesses of such a belief, according to him, is that it is impossible to prove one way or another.[5] But many would argue that the New Age Movement is now supplying the evidence. As entities are channeled in from all over the cosmos, the special effects departments in Hollywood provide an increasingly realistic backdrop to this belief, making it more possible than ever before for people to believe that they – or their film heroes – have actually come into personal contact with beings from out there. The fact that this belief is so deeply engrained in the mainstream of American culture, in particular, goes a long way towards explaining why, even in our cynical age, contact with extraterrestrial and spirit entities is still so eagerly embraced by so many as the answer to all our problems.

Most of us do not read the works of the American Transcendentalists, nor for that matter the writings of poets like Tennyson or Wordsworth. It takes a more popular movement to put this belief on the agenda of ordinary people. That is exactly what happened in a modest clapboard homestead in Hydesville, NY, which is where hands-on contact with the other world began in modern times. The farm cottage that now stands on the site is not the original, but a replica of the home in which John and Margaret Fox and their two daughters, Margaret and Kate, got in touch with the spirit world on 31 March 1848. After hearing a series of unusual banging noises in the wall of the house, the family decided to challenge whoever was making them to identify themselves. Something replied to their challenge, claiming to be the spirit of someone murdered there long before (a skeleton was indeed unearthed on the site half a century later). This disembodied spirit appeared to have uncanny knowledge of events in the Foxes' own lives. It knew the number and ages of John and Margaret's children – even the ones that had lived for only a short time. Within eighteen months the two daughters had become celebrities. Contacting the spirits of the dead became an American obsession, spreading throughout much of the country, and even across the Atlantic to England.

In the closing years of the nineteenth century, people were falling over themselves to get in touch with dead relatives, and there was no shortage of mediums claiming to be able to facilitate their search. One of the most famous was Helena Petrovna Blavatsky. Her early life in Russia was shrouded in mystery, but she claimed to have travelled the world before finally arriving in New York city on 7 July 1873. Once established in the USA, she set up the Brotherhood of Luxor. In 1875, with backing from an American named Henry Steel Olcott, this became known as the Theosophical Society. She was to attract the admiration of many of the influential people of her day, including the scientist Thomas Edison and the poets Yeats and Tennyson. Though she was involved in many aspects of spiritualism (as it came to be called), Blavatsky's main contribution was the idea that information could be channeled not so much from the spirits of those who were deceased, but from sources of cosmic wisdom. Following the establishment of her Theosophical Society, her aims were set out at great length in a 1,200-page book entitled *Isis Unveiled*. This was a channeled document 'dictated by the Masters of Wisdom via astral light and spirit guides'. Like today's New Age channelers, Blavatsky gave a personal identity to the source of many of her revelations. She claimed they emanated from an Indian by the name of Koot Hoomi Lal Singh, who had progressed through many reincarnations in order to accumulate such a vast store of cosmic wisdom. Though there were many unresolved questions about Blavatsky's claims, her message became very popular, especially among professional and upper-class people – an interesting foreshadowing of the New Age Movement, which draws its support from the same classes.

On into the early twentieth century, other influential characters emerged, also claiming to have the power to channel wisdom from cosmic masters. Among them was Alice Bailey, founder of the Arcane School, who produced twenty-five books between 1919 and 1949, allegedly containing the distilled wisdom of the Tibetan entity Djwhal Khul. Elizabeth Clare Prophet, present leader of the Church Universal and Triumphant, also claims to be the mouthpiece and channel for a select group of Ascended Masters. These astral gurus speak only to her and include Jesus, Mary, Pope John XIII, Sir Thomas More and the eighteenth-century mystic St Germaine. What they say is an interesting mystical mixture appealing mainly to conservative yuppies. In it, right-wing politics and American patriotism rub shoulders with various eastern and occult beliefs. The whole thing is spiced up with New Age jargon and selected aspects of a Christian-flavoured Gnosticism.

Edgar Cayce, who died in 1945, was another American mystic who did much to popularize belief in reincarnation. As a therapist, he specialized in psychic diagnosis of medical conditions, and one of his main healing techniques was what is now called past-life recall. But he was also a channeler for an entity which claimed to give scientific information as well as metaphysical insights. This is a procedure that still goes on today through the Center for Applied Intuition in San Francisco, where channelers try to use their psychic abilities to solve otherwise insoluble scientific problems. The Values and Lifestyle survey carried out by SRI International, based at the prestigious Stanford University, found that an amazing 57% of the mainstream scientific community apparently believes there could be something in it. At a more popular level, channelers William Rainan and Thomas Jacobson both regularly get in touch with 'Dr Peebles', an entity which claims to be a nineteenth-century Scots medic, who makes medical diagnoses as well as metaphysical revelations.

The New Age Movement has produced a fair number of well-known and highly esteemed channelers, whose powers are admired and frequently consulted. J. Z. Knight is just one of a vast number of people who manage to make a comfortable living through these activities. Others include Kevin Ryerson, who played a strategic part in Shirley Maclaine's spiritual awakening, and Jach Pursel, who channels an entity called Lazaris into the lives of many Hollywood stars. Most of these people first met their spirit guides by accident – and certainly with little, if any, prior preparation. J. Z. Knight, for example, first encountered Ramtha after she had spent a weekend exploring pyramid power in her kitchen at home. As she placed a pyramid on her head, mindful of the ancient legends that suggested it could be a powerful concentrator of cosmic and spiritual energy, she had an experience that changed the course of her life. In her own words, 'I blinked, and to my utter shock and amazement, there stood a giant man at the other end of my kitchen . . . just standing there, aglow . . . A smile so divine parted his lips to reveal glistening, immaculate teeth. "I am Ramtha, the Enlightened One. I have come to help you over the ditch."'[6] He went on to inform her that she and her family were in mortal danger, and should move house in order to survive. To cut a long story short, they did – and their original home was smashed up by a brutal gang not long after.

SPIRITUAL ANSWERS

Not surprisingly, many people who receive such revelations are suspicious and cynical when these entities make
the first moves to establish contact. But it is also possible
to learn how to channel by utilizing specific techniques
that will put you in touch with spiritual entities.
Sometimes these are connected with the psychological
techniques used for going within, in order to discover
yourself. Indeed, for New Agers the ultimate answer to
what you are is likely to be a spiritual answer of this kind.
For the main discovery to be made about yourself is that
you are not just – or mainly – flesh and bones: you are a
spiritual being. Knowing yourself includes knowledge of
who you have been (in past lives) as well as who you are
now, and who you may wish to be in the future. Spirit
guides are the ones who can answer such questions,
though these entities may also be identified with the
'Higher Self', the core of your spiritual being, also called
the superconscious, oversoul, God-Self or Christ-
Consciousness. Shirley Maclaine quotes a Swedish
friend as saying, 'We are all spiritual beings. We just
don't acknowledge it. We are spiritual beings of energy
who happen to be in the physical body at the present time
and Ambres [a channeled entity] is a spiritual being of
energy who does not happen to be in the body right now.
Of course, he is highly evolved, but then so are we. The
difference is that we don't believe it.'[7]

The Higher Self is the entity which can help you to
identify your own higher purpose. Through it, you
consciously chose to be here, and to be who you are –
which is why contact with it now can keep you focused on
your true life purposes. No wonder that those who find
life aimless and without purpose are so strongly attracted

to therapists who claim to be able to put them in touch with their spirit guides. Not only can they resolve uncertainties and questions about our present lives by reference back to what took place in past lives. But they also claim to be able to answer the big, ultimate questions, by giving us a fresh understanding of ourselves in relation to the whole cosmic scheme of things. There is an appealing and forceful message in all this, especially to people who suffer from a low self-esteem. For it suggests that you are actually a very powerful and important being, with the potential to do absolutely anything at all.

There can be no one alive who has not at some time wondered, Why am I here? A question which naturally leads to another, namely, Where did I come from? The New Age answer is simple: we are all souls in the process of being recycled – an attractive idea in itself to a generation committed to finding a solution to our environmental crisis. To the uninitiated, this may sound like Hinduism in a new western dress. But it is actually quite different. Hinduism believes that the form in which a soul returns is directly related to its moral performance in previous lives. New Agers, by contrast, claim that souls make personal choices as to who they will be, and what their circumstances will be. And they make the choice on the basis of their own perceived spiritual needs at any given point. In his book, *The Emerging New Age*, sociology professor J. L. Simmons puts it like this:

> . . . the decision to be reborn is self-determined by each being in consultation with familiar spirits and, often, a small group of more knowledgeable coun-sellors. The rebirth is planned . . . Such plans include the circumstances of birth and a blueprint outline of the life to follow, so that certain experiences

might provide the opportunity to learn certain lessons.[8]

This means that whoever you are, and whatever you experience, it happens to you because you choose that it will. Including deprivation, oppression and marginalization while you're alive, and for some, even a gruesome death:

> We create the realities we experience, consciously or unknowingly. The universe ultimately gives us what we ask for . . . Since we construct our own lives, it is false and misleading to blame others for what we are experiencing . . . The buck stops with us. And change is in our own hands.[9]

This is Hinduism deprived of its moral fibre. The eastern concept of reincarnation has been disembowelled, and combined with western individualism and basic human selfishness. A combination that gives you the best of all possible worlds: the safety and security of a belief system that promises eternal existence without any demand for moral responsibility. When leading New Age guru Bhagwan Shree Rajneesh ('Osho') died in January 1990, his ashes were installed in Pune, India, in a glass-panelled mausoleum that was once his bedroom. The marble container was embossed with an epitaph inscribed in gold, which said it all: 'Osho – never born, never died, visited the planet Earth between December 11 1931 and January 19 1990.' In other words, he'd never really been here. Which was just as well, for he once claimed to have had sex with more women than any other man in the entire history of the world, and following the 1985 collapse of his 'Big Muddy' commune in Oregon, he was deported from the USA and subsequently thrown out of no fewer than twenty-one other countries! It was later claimed that activities at the 'Big Muddy' included crimes that ranged from phonetapping to the mass poisoning of 700 people. But since he'd never really been here, presumably he was not responsible!

CHANNELING

What can we make of all this? Let's begin with channeling, for this seems to be the major source of this kind of teaching. Can we trust channeling to be what it claims to be? Are channelers crooks and charlatans? Or genuinely spiritual advisers? Or sincere, but deluded? Or even, perhaps, dangerous and demonic? This question has been floating round in the back of my mind ever since I first attended a New Age channeling session. Like most other questions about the New Age, there is no one simple answer to it. At the risk of over-simplifying things, I would suggest that modern channeling falls into at least four quite distinct categories.

There can be no doubt that a lot of fraudulent claims are being made, and some channelers are making money under false pretences. People are claiming to have received messages from extraterrestrial spirit guides, when they know perfectly well that no such thing has happened. This observation is hardly surprising, of course. You only need to recall the scandals that beset so many US tele-evangelists in the 1980s to realize that if there is a genuine market for a religious product, hucksters and cheats soon muscle in on the act. Spiritualism has been plagued by this throughout modern times. Even the Fox sisters who started it all eventually admitted that they had faked some of their early experiences, and one of them (Kate) ultimately turned her back on the whole business. It is always going to be difficult to distinguish fact from fiction in this area. *Caveat emptor!* – Let the buyer beware!

But not all consumers are being ripped off, even when the channeling is faked. A lot of people attend channeling sessions simply for entertainment. It's certainly not quite the same experience as an old-fashioned variety show, nor even a modern pop concert. But some channelers are neither more nor less than good actors and actresses, who are providing entertainment for a particular kind of paying audience. They know that, and the audience know it – and everybody gets a reasonable deal. This is especially true of some channelings I have attended in the USA, where there is a much lighter touch to it all than tends to be the case in Europe. Audiences treat it much the same way as they would with any kind of magic show. They know that what seems to be happening isn't quite the whole picture. But as long as it's a good show, who cares?

The second category gives more cause for concern. For some channelers I have met are almost certainly mentally unbalanced. We all know that believing you are somebody else can be a symptom of a wide range of psychiatric disturbances, and it has to be more than just coincidence that many channelers have been abused as children or have had difficult experiences, which would naturally predispose them to psychological and other problems. A fascinating case surfaced in August 1990 when a twenty-nine-year-old man from Oshkosh, Wisconsin, was charged with raping a local woman. A straightforward enough allegation, except that the woman claimed she was many different people. The defence argued that in one personality she had engaged voluntarily in sexual intercourse, and then when she changed personality a different identity felt she had been forced into it against her will. These personalities varied from a woman called 'Jennifer', who was a fun-loving, promiscuous twenty-year-old, to a much older woman named 'Franny' and a vulnerable six-year-old girl called 'Emily'. An expert witness claimed that the woman had as many as twenty-one different personalities, and identified this as a mental illness that typically develops after a traumatic childhood experience. The court certainly took it all seriously, and the District Attorney invited her to change personalities while on the witness stand – a request that she was quite able to comply with. Even more amazingly, Robert Hawley, the Winnebago County Circuit Judge, required the woman to take an oath each time she changed personalities. The lawyers then formally introduced themselves to the different personalities, assuming that such knowledge did not automatically transfer between them. All this is almost a carbon-copy of what takes place at many channeling sessions, where a channeler may typically claim to be tuning into messages from several different personalities, each of whom has his or her own tone of voice and makes personal introductions. Certainly, the similarities are too close to be coincidental. Those who denounce channeling unequivocally would do well to bear this in mind, and to realize that a number of totally innocent and unbalanced people are locked in there, frequently being manipulated by others who merely use them to their own advantage.

If these two categories were the only things involved in channeling, you might wonder what all the fuss is about. But in other cases something unusual definitely is happening – though not so much related to contact with beings who are 'out there', as tuning in to material already locked away in the psyche of the channeler. Most channelers begin their sessions with something that looks very much like a form of self-hypnosis, and deliver their messages while in a state of trance – frequently claiming later that they have no idea what they said while in this condition. It is of course widely recognized that we are conscious of only a tiny percentage of all the material locked away in our brains, and there are many well-known techniques for accessing the rest of it. This process is not necessarily dangerous in itself, and is part of the stock-in-trade of all conventional psychiatrists and psychologists. What is potentially dangerous is the induction of a trance-like state in oneself, and many of the tapes and records produced for this purpose can raise genuine concerns for the health and safety of those who use them. In any event, the messages delivered in this form of trance channeling are generally predictable and self-affirming. Not surprising, perhaps, because what comes out is what was already there. Such messages typically reinforce and back-up particular lifestyles, and generally reassure their recipients that they are at the centre of things, and are on the right track and have little to fear.

It is impossible to overestimate the creative capacity of the human imagination, and probably the majority of New Age channeling – and the personalities who claim to be speaking through it – emanate from this source. However, this is not the whole story. In his classic book, *The Screwtape Letters*, Oxford academic C. S. Lewis made a very perceptive comment about all this. Two devils are planning their strategy:

> Our policy, for the moment, is to conceal ourselves. Of course this has not always been so. We are really faced with a cruel dilemma. When the humans disbelieve in our existence we lose all the pleasing results of direct

terrorism, and we make no magicians. On the other hand, when they believe in us, we cannot make them materialists and sceptics. At least, not yet. I have great hopes that we shall learn in due time how to emotionalize and mythologize their science to such an extent that what is, in effect, a belief in us (though not under that name) will creep in while the human mind remains closed to belief in the Enemy. The 'Life Force', the worship of sex and some aspects of Psychoanalysis may here prove useful. If once we can produce our perfect work – the Materialist Magician, the man, not using, but veritably worshipping, what he vaguely calls 'Forces' while denying the existence of 'spirits' – then the end of the war will be in sight.[10]

There can be no doubt that Lewis was envisaging a time when the non-threatening and seemingly scientific language of psychology would be used as a cover for occult and demonic activities. Whether or not he was right in his analysis is perhaps open to question, but channeling certainly blurs the edges between these two aspects of human experience. Alice Bailey, for example, claimed that something like 85% of channeled messages come from within the channeler's own subconscious mind. But that still leaves another 15% that presumably comes from some other force or influence outside and beyond the channeler's own personal frame of reference. There can be no doubt that mixed up in all this are techniques and experiences that in other circumstances would be labelled the occult. It is important not to exaggerate this, however. The majority of New Agers are not consciously dabbling with the occult all the time – and if they thought this was where it was leading, they would be the first to back off. From my own experience of alleged channelings of spirit guides, I would estimate that no more than about 20% of them are specifically and self-consciously occult experiences. So it is important to keep a sense of proportion here. There is less of the occult in it than many western Christians are claiming. But equally, New Agers who deny it is there are gullible and naive. The least we can say is that those who are involved in this whole phenomenon are likely to make contact with sinister movements and possibilities that they would not otherwise have encountered. And when leading Satanists have gone on record as saying that the New Age Movement – while not the 'real thing' from their point of view – is softening people up to be more open to satanic involvement, it would be foolish and shortsighted to ignore them. This is often down-played or ignored, particularly in the popular presentation of the New Age Movement found in glossy magazines and TV programmes. But to do so is a serious mistake. By all means let us recognize that the New Age vacuum cleaner – to return to the imagery used in Chapter 1 – contains many things that are harmless, and maybe even fun. But there is also in there a hard core of danger that we overlook at our peril. Contact with spirit guides is not always the wholesome and benevolent experience many people imagine. This is something we will follow up shortly.

REINCARNATION

Belief in reincarnation is the bottom line on which this entire worldview depends. If we are not spirits continually being recycled, then the idea that there are spirit guides out there waiting to give us advice makes little sense. That wouldn't necessarily prevent people from believing in it all, of course, for one of the hallmarks of the New Age Movement is the assumption that things do not need to make rational sense in order to be true. But what about reincarnation? Notwithstanding the remarkable growth of New Age thinking in the last ten years, it is still the case that most western scientists and religious believers deny that there is such a thing as past lives. Others disagree, and claim to be in possession of evidence to back up their views. It has to be said, however, that even the sympathetic observer is forced to admit that much of the so-called evidence is unreliable, and all of it is, at best, circumstantial. But reincarnation is so widely believed in today that it is worthwhile here to review the subject. Three claims are typically made.

1. Intelligent people believe in it

It is often claimed that many great people of the past have believed in reincarnation, even those completely untouched by eastern mysticism – from ancient Greek philosophers and scientists such as Pythagoras, Euclid and Plato, to modern American heroes like Benjamin Franklin, Thomas Edison, Mark Twain and Abraham Lincoln – not to forget European thinkers such as Leibnitz, Hegel and Goethe, as well as mystical traditions in many world religions. There are a couple of problems with this frequently repeated claim. First, it is not unequivocally certain that all these people did actually believe in reincarnation – and those who claim they did often need to resort to unconvincing arguments. For example, when J. L. Simmons colourfully characterizes Pythagoras as 'actually a wacked-out mystic',[11] he fails to point out that there is absolutely no solid basis of fact in such a description. Secondly, the fact that famous people happen to hold a particular belief is scarcely sufficient reason for concluding that it must be true. History is littered with eccentrics who believed all sorts of bizarre things – and their judgements need to be scrutinized as carefully as anyone else's. They could all be wrong, and the fact that they were either famous or successful is totally irrelevant.

2. Surprising experiences

Other evidence should be taken more seriously, but at the end of the day it too is inconclusive. Near-death experiences – which are merely a particular type of out-of-body experience – play a major role here. A typical example would be a terminally ill patient in hospital under medical care. Some kind of physical crisis might arise – difficult breathing, cardiac arrest, or the like – in which the patient appears to external observers to be completely unconscious. On the contrary, however, the patient herself actually has a heightened sense of consciousness – though not in the body. The patient may find her true self apparently leaving the body, maybe watching from the ceiling what is happening as medics try to revive it. She is strangely conscious that she belongs to the body – or vice versa – but is not connected to it. Others talk of this kind of experience in slightly different terms. They find themselves floating down a dark tunnel, with a bright light at the end of it. They emerge from the far end of the tunnel, and they are in a beautiful, near-perfect, light-filled place. A place populated by others whom they may recognize as friends or relatives. Perhaps there is a river or some gates through which they are invited to go. They choose not to go through, and they have a sensation of returning to their physical body. Whether this is how death actually is, who knows?

It would be foolish to deny that these experiences are real. They have been reported so frequently, at all historical periods, that we must take them seriously. I remember that when I was a child, probably about ten or twelve years old, my uncle had a classic experience of this kind while undergoing a surgical operation for stomach ulcers. It was a talking point for years, and I remember quizzing him about it on many occasions. He had no doubt at all that something both real and profound had happened to him. But what was it? Many medical scientists describe such experiences as some kind of hallucination caused by oxygen deprivation at critical points in the course of illness or crisis – an opinion that may or may not be correct, but which we need not consider at this point. For supposing there is some more profound, even spiritual, explanation for them, does that then prove reincarnation? The answer must clearly be no. My own uncle was certain that his experience provided evidence of survival after death and the existence of a spiritual realm. But reincarnation would be a stage further on, and the links simply do not exist to go that far. Even to get as far as we have, one needs to make a lot of assumptions that may easily turn out to be completely unjustified. It is surely significant that at the end of her comprehensive and well-researched book, Carol Zaleski finally concludes with these words:

> Otherworld visions are products of the same imaginative power that is active in our ordinary ways of visualizing death; our tendency to portray ideas in concrete, embodied, and dramatic forms; the capacity of our inner states to transfigure our perception of outer landscapes . . . and our drive to experience that

universe as a moral and spiritual cosmos in which we belong and have a purpose. Whatever the study of near-death visions might reveal about the experience of death, it teaches us just as much about ourselves as image-making and image-bound beings.[12]

3. Past-life recall

Life after death is one thing – but what about life before birth? From time to time, stories are unearthed of people who not only claim to have lived before, but who can remember exactly who they were in a previous life and can describe all sorts of details of that past existence. Their memories of their past lives vary from merely having a hunch that they've been in a place before or that they've already met someone they don't actually know, to knowing quite specific details of personal relationships or even of previous deaths. It has even been claimed that the phenomenon of 'child prodigies' can be explained by the supposition that particular skills were learned in previous lives. So Mozart, for example, was not particularly gifted: he'd just been around for a long time, cosmically speaking. However, there is no evidence that either he or any other western child prodigy has ever claimed to remember a previous existence. As a transpersonal psychologist once said to me when he knew I was a published author: 'Maybe you were once Shakespeare, or one of the Bible writers, I don't know. But you've got to be an old soul – about 30,000 years old, I guess.' I suppose that was meant to be a compliment.

It is in fact transpersonal psychology that has brought this whole issue to the fore in recent discussion of the subject. For past-life recall has become a major technique among New Age therapists. The theory is straightforward. If you have a problem here and now for which there is no immediately obvious explanation in your present life experience, the chances are that you're suffering some kind of hang-up from the traumas of a past existence. You can't get on with your boss? Maybe you had a real life-or-death struggle with him in a previous life. You don't like spiders? Well, it's always possible you were killed by a poisonous variety at another time and place. Going back to those other times and places should sort out your feelings and put you on the right track for understanding yourself now, and living your present life in a more fulfilled way.

Most of us do not spontaneously have such an awareness. Indeed, past-life therapists generally claim that it is only children up to the age of about three years who are likely to. For the rest of us, some kind of drug- or hypnosis-induced trance state is necessary before we can access our cosmic memory banks. There can be no doubt that under such conditions many people behave as if they were someone else, apparently adopting different personalities. But such procedures are not without risk, and it is not unknown for this alternative personality to refuse to go away when instructed by the therapist, leaving people in altered states of personality for days or even weeks. In addition, mainline psychiatrists are divided in their opinions of what is actually happening in these instances. Hypnotism itself is a dream-like state, in which the subconscious mind is released from its normal inhibitions, and the therapist assumes a dominant position. When specific suggestions are made to people in this state, they can – and often do – fantasize specifically to please the hypnotist, and all kinds of hidden desires may emerge spontaneously in the form of an imaginary personality. In such a state descriptions of places, people and artefacts can indeed be very vivid, for hypnotized subjects invariably have a very graphic picture of whatever the hypnotist suggests. We do not need to decide whether this kind of explanation is correct. But the fact that there is so much genuine disagreement on the matter should at least alert us to the fact that we are handling a whole collection of phenomena that need to be carefully appraised.

Other understandings of past-life recall range from the fanciful to the merely rationalistic. Some see all this kind of activity as demonic, and believe that under hypnotic conditions people can be possessed by spirits – either evil spirits or restless spirits that actually belong to personalities who once lived. Others try to explain it by reference to poltergeist activity. While yet others think there is a simple, non-supernatural explanation. Back in the 1950s Edwin Zolik, then a psychology professor at Marquette University in the USA, became interested in the subject. He studied many people in a state of such hypnotic regression, and came to the conclusion that the imagined 'past lives' were actually constructed out of materials that they were unconsciously familiar with (films, books and so on), and that they were essentially fantasies through which the personality disorders of the present were being worked out. The fact that there is a high incidence of violent and gruesome deaths among those who claim to remember past lives perhaps reinforces the view that the phenomenon is related to the working out of present tensions rather than the recollection of previous existence. In other words, like a lot of channeling, what comes out is what is already there – but hidden deep in the unconscious psyche. This view does not try to deny the therapeutic value of this kind of experience for some people – but it does put a serious question-mark against the idea that past-life recall is evidence for reincarnation.

It is not hard to understand why people long for a second chance in life. If you have a humdrum existence now, you will certainly get a kick out of believing you were once truly important. Your self-confidence will take a big leap if you learn that you have previously been an Egyptian princess, or an American president, or a famous religious leader. But so many people have claimed to be Buddha, Jesus Christ and Mary Queen of Scots that they can't all be right!

MORALITY

Speculation about past lives may be an interesting diversion. But this whole way of looking at things poses far more serious problems that impinge on our experience of life here and now. We have already characterized this as Hinduism deprived of its moral basis, and for many thinking and sensitive people, this is precisely the problem with it. In classical Hindu thought, reincarnation has an ethical basis: the form in which you return will be determined by the way you have lived previously. To use Christian imagery, you reap what you sow. *Karma*, in Hindu terminology. But New Agers believe we actually choose our own *karma*! Professor Simmons again:

> This is not some sort of Cosmic Justice, handed down by a God or the Fates. Instead, it is a matter of imagination and vibration levels. What we think and do . . . sets into motion what we experience, then and later.[13]

To put it simply, what this means is that I need have no sense of moral responsibility for anyone else except

myself. You don't need to be particularly sensitive to see
that the belief that we are who we want to be can have
disastrous knock-on effects for others in the wider
community. As a matter of fact, most of our present
world crises – whether social, ecological, human or
natural – have been created precisely by that kind of
mind-set. To suppose that the disadvantaged, marginalized and exploited people of today's world have chosen to
be that way is not only arrogant and selfish, it is the
ultimate blasphemy against human nature. It means that
the western yuppie can sit in the comfort of his luxury
limousine and drive past a family squatting in a cardboard
box, with not the slightest twinge of conscience. He has
chosen to be rich and prosperous. They – for some totally
incomprehensible reason – have chosen to be poor and
homeless. He might not understand why they have
decided to live in that state. But he need not doubt that
they are there by their own free choice – presumably to
fulfil some weird spiritual need that the rest of us can
scarcely begin to comprehend. The only thing that is
certain is that since that is their choice, no one else need
feel obliged to intervene!

I remember giving a lecture on the New Age
Movement in the Western Australian city of Perth, in the
course of which I identified this attitude as one of the
major weaknesses of New Age thinking. Imagine my
surprise when the leader of a New Age organization leapt
up afterwards and assured me that though I had fairly
described what he believed, this was no weakness – it was
a strength. When pressed further in discussion, he went
so far as to affirm that suffering blacks in South Africa,
and even victims of the Nazi Holocaust, were there as a
result of their own choices, which in turn were related to
their personal spiritual goals. I could hardly believe my

ears. And I believe the vast majority of ordinary people around the world would be as horrified as I was. But this lack of moral integrity is the logical outcome of the New Age worldview. Writing of the horrific ritual killings perpetrated by American mass murderer Charles Manson and his associates, Oxford scholar R. C. Zaehner has no hesitation in tracing them back directly to this kind of outlook. 'Charles Manson,' he says, 'was absolutely sane: he had been *there*, where there is neither good nor evil . . . If the ultimate truth . . . is that "All is One" and "One is All" . . . then have we any right to blame Charles Manson? For seen from the point of view of the eternal Now, he *did* nothing at all.'[14]

These are uncomfortable facts for the New Age Movement, which is why they are usually conveniently ignored. But how can we take seriously an outlook claiming to be committed to a holistic world vision, when it takes such a selfish stand on social ethics? The sad fact is that, unless social problems impinge directly on our own lives, it is all too easy for us to pretend that they do not exist. Writing of the Gulf War, *Boston Globe* columnist Mike Barnicle put his finger on our problem: 'Our culture is rooted in instant gratification, quick rewards at bargain-basement prices. If the cost is heavy, or the road a bit long, recent history shows we would rather take an early exit. The nation wallows in a tidal pool of huge debt, enormous self-pity and incredible selfishness.' And the New Age outlook panders to it.

SOCIAL JUSTICE

Which brings us on to a final compelling reason for placing a big question mark against all this. The worldview which is presented here is basically animistic, magical, pagan – and socially regressive. As New Agers love to point out, it was once the dominant worldview of many different societies. But its gradual displacement by other outlooks has not been a mistake: it has come about for very good reasons. For this is the outlook that has consistently produced some of the most oppressive forms of social organization that the world has ever seen. Societies in which women have been regularly abused, children have on occasion been sacrificed, and a small number of people claiming superior spiritual knowledge have terrified everybody else. Those voices that are now raised so insistently in the West – especially in the environmental movement – telling us there is ancient wisdom locked away in the traditions of obscure tribal peoples would do well to ponder the undeniable fact that there is frequently a black side to what they are advocating. In spite of all the high-sounding theorizing going on in some allegedly enlightened circles today, the fact is that wherever it has been the dominant social force, this kind of worldview has not historically led to a holistic lifestyle, or equality for women, or peaceful co-existence. Quite the reverse. There is a lot of unjustified and naive euphoria and optimism among westerners encountering all this for the first time.

The entities channeled in New Age seances are all charmingly positive and beneficial. An ad for a channeling course puts it so well: 'Channeling is a powerful and exciting way to discover the higher purpose in your life. Following your higher purpose will bring great gifts of joy, aliveness, and self-love. The ability to connect with a high level guide is a skill that can be learned easily and joyfully. Therefore, the goal of this course is to create a conscious link with your guide so you can channel higher guidance of love and light, thus empowering yourself and others.' J. L. Simmons says the essential characteristic of such spirits is to be 'playful'. It all sounds so agreeable that anyone would wish to have a go. But this is a deceptively pleasant way of looking at it – for only a fool would forget that there is also what has been called the 'left-hand path', in which more malevolent forces are at work. To be fair, we should note that some New Agers are aware of this. Writing in *Gnosis* for winter 1990, Richard Smoley cautions, 'we have no assurance that an entity is wiser, more loving, or more knowledgeable simply because it is from another realm . . . Christian literature has a long tradition of the "discernment of Spirits". Perhaps it is one that deserves more attention.'[15] But a more common New Age reaction is to play down this element. J. L. Simmons again: 'There are no actual demons as such, but trafficking with less evolved beings and the low levels of the astral planes engenders little joy or light or love . . . To put it mildly, the lower astral levels are not as pleasant as the higher ones . . .'[16] The fact that he uses colourful language to describe such beings ('more a spiritual skid row than . . . the hell of traditional religions') masks the impact that such encounters can have. Other New Agers are far more realistic about the likely outcome of such dealings with 'low-level spirits'. In his book, *Journeys out of the Body*, experienced astral traveller Robert Monroe recalls an occasion when he was repeatedly and viciously attacked by what he identified as evil spirits, two of whom changed into images of his daughters in an effort to unbalance him as he fought against them.[17] The number of adverts for 'spirit entity releasement' appearing in New Age magazines should also sound some warning bells. One ad asks, 'Have you ever been involved with drugs, alcoholism, channeling, or have difficulty with meditation, poor concentration, memory problems, hear voices, or have recurring dreams or nightmares? Do you feel that something is influencing your life? These symptoms could indicate that one or more disincarnate entities are influencing you.' It goes on to explain that 'Many spirits upon dying do not make it through the portal back into the light and the transition place. They remain, instead, earthbound, and attach to a living human as an energy source, often bringing profound change and chaos in the personality of the host person.' It warns that 'Common places where entities are likely to attach include bars, hospitals, scenes of accidents, or death. Sexual intercourse, substance abuse, or any traumatic event opens up the aura and allows you to be vulnerable to attachment.' Change one or two words in there, and you could easily be hearing a Christian warning against involvement in the demonic and the occult.

It is worth emphasizing here that most people who become involved in the New Age Movement have no interest in getting tangled up with this kind of thing. They are honest people, searching for honest answers to their own and the world's predicament. But they are often also naive and gullible people. They would never trust a stranger, yet fall over themselves to receive and act upon messages from channeled entities whose identity and integrity is at best questionable. The fact is that once you begin to mess about with this sort of thing, it is all too easy to be drawn into more sinister commitments. This may not be the user-friendly face of the New Age that is promoted in glossy brochures. But it cannot be denied that it is there. I remember visiting a sociology professor in Berkeley, California, who was not himself a New Ager, but had given testimony in a number of lawsuits involving the subject. I have never met a person so paranoid as he was. He found it impossible to believe I was who I claimed to be, and was certain that I had been sent from the Mafia or some other organized crime ring to beat him up. As a result, he was constantly armed, and obviously ready to use his weapons – even in a university office. He didn't need to tell me that he'd encountered the dark side of the New Age.

Others have met it when innocently joining New Age seminars and workshops. A young woman of Jewish extraction went to a residential course in England, and during it was the subject of a vicious physical assault. She naturally complained to the course organizers. And their response? 'You brought your own negative *karma* with you by choosing to have Jewish ancestry.' J. L. Simmons appears to support such an understanding of human existence when he writes: 'Different ethnic groups literally create and inhabit different worlds within the larger planetary sphere. We are all performers in the melodramas we have co-created and staged.'[18]

Those who know the teachings of some of the historical predecessors of today's New Age Movement will not be taken aback by this. Helena Blavatsky was deeply anti-Semitic, and Lanz von Liebenfels' 'Ariosophy', which stemmed directly from Blavatsky's Theosophy, was a strong influence in the creation of Hitler's Nazi ideology. Alice Bailey too – though she took a strongly anti-Nazi stance – nevertheless described the Jews as 'the world's worst problem' because, as she put it in her book *The Problems of Humanity* (written in 1947, after the Holocaust!), 'separateness' is 'the source of all evil'.[19] This is an opinion that is widely held by today's New Agers. In his book *Revelation: the birth of a New Age* David Spangler comments that those who oppose the New Age ideology will ultimately have to be

eliminated if and when the New Age society arrives.[20]
Reflecting on what this could mean, Dr Margaret
Brearley – who is Senior Research Fellow at the Centre
for Judaism and Jewish-Christian Relations in Bir-
mingham, England, and hardly an extremist – has no
hesitation in describing the New Age as 'a potential new
Holocaust'.[21]

It would be wrong to imply that all New Agers advocate
violence in support of their cause. Many who find
themselves generally attracted to the New Age worldview
are horrified when they first come across this side of it. In
addition, the fact that New Age thinking can on occasion
lead to racial discrimination and strong-arm tactics
makes it neither better nor worse than other contemporary world religions. Western Christians in particular
have little room to throw stones at this point, and should
never forget it. They too have frequently lost their way
and denied their spiritual heritage, as we shall see in our
final chapter. Before we get there, however, we have
some other meandering paths to explore. For the history
of channeling is closely tied up with the rapidly growing
interest in alternative medicine, and to complete the
picture this is where we now turn.

Chapter 5

HEALING – OURSELVES AND OUR ENVIRONMENT

SOME time ago, a couple whom I had known off and on for several years came to see me. They must have been in their mid-fifties, I suppose, and the man had just been diagnosed as a cancer sufferer. It had come to him literally out of the blue, and not surprisingly, they were both extremely distressed about it. Question marks now hung over all the things they had been planning for the future, while the past was scrupulously searched for possible clues that could explain why this had happened to them.

As we talked it all through, it soon became obvious that the cancer itself – horrific though it was – was not their most immediate concern at that particular moment. For instead of focusing on the physical symptoms of the disease, almost the whole conversation centred on the doctors whom they had visited in the course of the preceding two or three weeks. One doctor in particular: a radiologist who had performed a body scan to find out what was going on. It had been traumatic enough going to have the scan, and the fact that the results took another day or two to process only served to intensify what was already an emotionally charged situation. When the couple went to the doctor's office to be given his expert prognosis, they were already under an enormous amount of pressure. Being realistic people, they had prepared themselves to come to terms with the result, whatever it might be. But they were completely taken aback by what happened that day. Ushered into the medical inner sanctum, they met a man who looked everywhere except in their direction – who was either incapable of making eye contact with them, or else chose not to do so. He delivered his opinion in a single sentence: 'This is a real mess – the cancer's already well into your bone structure.' To which the hapless patient could only respond, 'This is bad news, then?' But by now the medic had done his job, and was already clearing his desk to move on to the next case. With a brisk assurance that they could expect to receive his account through the mail shortly, the doctor brought the interview to an abrupt end. So far as he was concerned, his job was done. But for the patient and his partner, this was only just the beginning. Dazed and embarrassed, they left the hospital in tears. At a time when they were acutely vulnerable, a so-called expert in health care had not only failed to offer them any real care and counsel, but had adopted such an offhand attitude that they felt personally assaulted – mentally and emotionally, if not physically.

Stories like that could be multiplied thousands of times over. Faced with the impersonal nature, the expense, the élitism – and, often, the ineffectiveness – of modern medical science, is it any wonder that many people feel something is wrong? When clinical efficiency, pay cheques and patient hours seem to be the only things that matter, what has happened to the high ideals of the Hippocratic oath and medical ethics? Not all medics are like this, of course. But the fact that any of them are is a powerful indictment of the educational system that has produced them. While the fact that such people can keep their jobs – even being promoted to top positions – is itself a sad comment on the priorities of the health care establishment.

Doctors have never had a good press. As long ago as the fourth century BC, Alexander the Great complained, 'I am dying with the help of too many physicians.' Today more than ever before, people are taking it for granted that if they want to be truly healthy, then the last place to go for assistance will be the doctor's office. We do not need to look far to find out why. Western medical education has historically been based on the same materialistic and reductionist principles as the rest of the scientific establishment. As a result of the all-pervasive influence of Enlightenment rationalism, two beliefs have predominated. The first is that the only things worth knowing are things you can think about. This means that anything that cannot be quantified rationally – such as the emotions – will automatically be given a lower status than the 'hard facts' of scientific analysis. The second belief is that you understand how things work by taking them apart. As a result, anatomy and physiology are central to medical science. This encourages doctors to proceed on the unspoken assumption that a patient is little more than a collection of spare parts that still happens to be breathing. Increasing specialization means that more doctors are sharing ever-expanding information about ever-smaller bits of the body. They find themselves untrained for, and therefore unsympathetic to, any aspects of human illness that transcend the narrow boundaries of their own primary interests. As a result, patients find that their doctors either misunderstand or play down their pain. They say there is nothing wrong, or that it is 'just their nerves'. And the closer the pain comes to the emotions and feelings, the greater the problem seems to be. Many doctors feel distinctly uncomfortable in handling emotions, whether their own or those of the patient. In my experience, it is highly unusual for a medic acting 'professionally' even to shake hands or make eye contact, let alone engage in any kind of body language that might conceivably communicate a message of care of compassion to the patients. The studied 'laying off of hands' seems to be one of their major therapeutic instruments, and even those who would like to be different find it impossibly threatening to institute change. It is easy to identify some of the causes of this sad state of affairs, and here the structure of traditional medical education must certainly have a lot to answer for. As Marilyn Ferguson says, 'Warmth, intuition, and imagination are precisely the characteristics likely to be screened out by the emphasis on scholastic standing and test scores. The right brain, in effect, was being denied admission to medical school. There were no quotas for creativity.'[1]

NEW PATHS TO HEALING

The domination of traditional health care by this mechanistic approach to people and their problems is a major reason for the rapid growth of 'alternative' or 'complementary' medicine. This is probably the one place where most people first encounter the New Age. They may not realize they're meeting New Age concepts, for in today's alternative market-place you can just as easily find old-fashioned herbal remedies as techniques such as acupuncture, crystal healing, colour balancing, channeling, psychic healing of the astral body and other therapies that are obviously 'different'. But none of it is truly new. Fringe medicine has been popular in the West for the last hundred years or so, and in addition it has generally thrived most vigorously within the evangelical Christian community – particularly among fringe groups such as Seventh Day Adventists or Plymouth Brethren, who have always had a suspicion of the establishment line, in medicine as in other areas of life. This is why some of the most heated debates about the New Age Movement among Christians have centred on alternative therapies. Practices that have been around for a long time have suddenly had the label 'New Age' stuck onto them, and treatments that may or may not have worked – but were certainly never believed to be deeply religious in any sense – have been scrutinized from new angles.

Many people with no connexion at all with the New Age Movement would readily agree with Shirley Maclaine when she says that 'natural, holistic approaches worked better for me than medicines or drugs. . . Orthodox Western medicine relied far too heavily on drugs.'[2] As a result, she and thousands of others are turning to techniques which are claimed to work in a completely different way. Instead of interfering from the outside with the body's natural workings – whether by drugs or surgery – alternative healers work from the inside, releasing the body's own natural healing energies to bring balance and wholeness and create a sense of spontaneous well-being.

The sceptic might be inclined to think this is all right for people who have never suffered from any major life-threatening illness. But others claim that even things like cancer can be contained – cured, perhaps – by these same methods. Another Hollywood actress, Jill Ireland, described her own experience:

I recalled the moment when I learned I had cancer. At the instant I heard those fateful words, something in me had kicked over. It was as if a switch had been thrown. I felt myself gather all my forces and begin to fight. The energy was there waiting to be tapped. It knew what to fight. The enemy was within my body. The question was how.

I also grasped the healing properties of quartz crystals for focusing and energizing my mind and body. A crystal is the only thing in the world that has a perfect molecular order; it is, in fact, perfect order. Sue Colin [her health adviser] used them for healing. She would hold a crystal in her hand, drawing the healing energy into her. Sometimes when I was with her, I would meditate using the energy of the crystal [and] held them during my cancer meditation.[3]

Utilizing such psychic energies to achieve a state of personal wholeness is obviously very different from the mechanistic approach of the scientific establishment. Even when alternative practitioners disclaim any spiritual dimension to their work, their assumptions are so obviously congenial to the New Age outlook that it is not hard to see why the two movements have become so closely interconnected. For spiritually starved westerners, the search for health has in some cases become a religion. In one of the most widely researched histories of the subject, American professor R. C. Fuller explains why:

metaphysical healing systems are almost perfectly suited to the secular character of our age in that they provide experiential access to the sacred while neatly sidestepping modern disquietude concerning traditional religious authority. In this way they initiate individuals otherwise quite at home in the modern world into a distinctively religious vision of the forces upon which health and happiness depend . . . *So prominent are the religious overtones of the healing movements that it is tempting to think that they function only secondarily as purveyors of therapeutic techniques . . .*[4]

ALTERNATIVE MEDICINE AND ESOTERIC SPIRITUALITY

In modern times, spiritual and religious 'awakenings' have regularly given birth to new concepts of health and medicine. The therapies that are enjoying renewed popularity today all have their origins with people and events we have met before in our discussion of the esoteric aspects of the New Age outlook. Swedenborg's New Jerusalem Church, Ellen G. White's Seventh Day Adventists and Mary Baker Eddy's Christian Science all feature prominently in the development of modern holistic health care. It is therefore no surprise to find that religious and metaphysical considerations play a key role in the practice of alternative medicine. In so far as alternative medicine requires a religious worldview, it undoubtedly finds the outlook of the New Age Movement a good deal more congenial than the theology of traditional mainstream Christianity.

We can trace the precursors of New Age therapies back to the experiments of Franz Anton Mesmer (1734–1815). A native of Vienna, he came up with the idea of 'animal magnetism' (that is, the union of body, mind and spirit). He believed that this was a medium through which forces of all kinds passed as they moved from one object to another. Light, heat, electricity and magnetism all operated through this energy network. A proper supply of 'animal magnetism' was essential for good health. Any kind of illness indicated that these forces had somehow become unbalanced, and so the restoration of balance was the key to healing. To achieve this balance of forces, Mesmer used various hypnotic techniques to produce altered states of consciousness in his patients – a practice which introduced the word 'mesmerize' into the English language. With the patient in this state, the therapist could concentrate the flow of 'animal magnetism' to diseased organs by passing his hands over the body or by using physical massage and manipulation.

This general idea that health is related to the balance of life-giving forces and energies, and that illness means that things are out of balance, is central to the majority of today's alternative therapies. Some therapists are concerned only with the balance of purely physical powers, such as the influence of magnetic force fields, but the concept is unquestionably rooted more in spiritual and mystical ideas from both East and West. The idea that everything and everybody is part of one universal cosmic energy system has provided a basis for the healing work of shamans and witch-doctors in all primal cultures, while the balancing of impersonal energy forces – *Chi* to the Chinese, *Ki* to the Japanese, *prana* to the Hindus – is the starting-point for all eastern mystical healing. In this view of things, pain is merely the accumulation of energy in the wrong place, and balancing the energy and shifting it round into the right places will restore health and harmony to the body. Writing as long ago as 1847, one George Bush observed that mesmerized people 'speak as if, to their consciousness, they had undergone an inward translation by which they had passed out of a material into a spiritual body. . . The state into which a subject is brought by the mesmerizing process is a state in which the spirit predominates for the time being over the body.'[5]

Other incidents from the same period enable us to trace explicit connexions between such alternative therapies and leading lights in the development of spiritualism, one of the streams that has flowed into the New Age Movement. In 1843, the mesmerist practitioner J. Stanley Grimes arrived in Poughkeepsie, the hometown of a humble American apprentice cobbler by the name of Andrew Jackson Davis. Grimes selected Davis at random at a public demonstration of his healing techniques, whereupon the cobbler soon found himself channeling messages from spirit guides, including the dead Emanuel Swedenborg who, it was claimed, was even wiser in the spirit than he had been in the flesh. He eventually wrote a book called *The Harmonial Philosophy*, a volume of health advice, much of it channeled from spirit guides, and all of it based on a spiritualist worldview. In a direct foreshadowing of today's New Age therapies, he clearly identified opening oneself up to greater spiritual powers as the key to good health.

The early history of osteopathy provides other examples of the same idea. It was founded by Andrew Taylor Still (1828-1917), the son of a Methodist minister who started his healing career as a magnetic mesmerist. He agreed that health was the harmonious and undisturbed flow of energy, but he also believed that blockages to this flow could be removed by manual manipulation of the body. He suggested:

'Think of yourself as an electric battery. Electricity seems to have the power to explode or distribute oxygen, from which we receive the vitalizing benefits. When it plays freely all through your system, you feel

well. Shut it off in one place and congestion may
result; in this case a medical doctor, by dosing you with
drugs, would increase this congestion until it resulted
in decay... Not so with an Osteopath. He removes the
obstruction, lets the life-giving current have full play,
and the man is restored to health.'[6]

This might seem merely a curiosity of the prescientific
mentality, except that Still also advised his patients to
'Remember that all power is powerless except the
unerring Deity of your being, to whose unchangeable
laws you must conform if you hope to win the battle of
your life.'[7]

Emanuel Swedenborg's religious ideas provided a
coherent frame of reference for the developing interests
of alternative practitioners. Relatively few of them
followed his teachings in detail. But his basic concepts
provided a structure within which a spiritual dimension
to life could be located. In particular, his view was that the
universe consisted of many inter-connecting dimensions
– physical, mental, spiritual, angelic and so on. It was
soon being argued that when harmony was established
between these realms, balance and wisdom could flow
from the higher into the lower. Therefore as the barriers
separating people from their cosmic context were broken
down, so wholeness and vitality would automatically be
induced. Therapies like this enjoyed great popularity
among the American Transcendentalists. People like
Henry David Thoreau and Ralph Waldo Emerson were
not only advocates of eastern mysticism: they were also
ardent devotees of alternative medicine. This view
expressed by nineteenth-century healer Ralph Waldo
Trine could have come straight from a modern New Age
manual:

In just the degree that we come into a conscious realization of our oneness with the Infinite Life, and open ourselves to the Divine inflow, do we actualize in ourselves the qualities and powers of the Infinite Life, do we make ourselves channels through which the Infinite Intelligence and Power can work. In just the degree in which you realize your oneness with the Infinite Spirit, you will exchange dis-ease for ease, inharmony for harmony, suffering and pain for abounding health and strength.[8]

Other pioneers in the field included John H. Kellogg. Originally a member of the Seventh Day Adventist Church, he soon abandoned orthodox Christian theology for the more esoteric beliefs that he recognized to be the only logical underpinning for the alternative health scene. Writing in 1903, he too expressed views that would readily be accepted within the New Age: 'God is *in* nature. . . God actually entered into the product of his creative skill, so that it might not only outwardly reflect the divine conception, but that it might think divinely, and act divinely.'[9] An opinion for which he was thrown out of the Seventh Day Adventist Church. (Incidentally, he also founded the breakfast cereal manufacturing company which still bears his name.) But he was not the only one to express such sentiments. Phineas Parkhurst Quimby (1802-1866) was another popular practitioner who proceeded along the same lines, arguing that 'all sickness is in the mind or belief. . . Disease is the effect of a wrong direction given to the mind. . . disease is something made by belief or forced upon us by our parents or public opinion. . . if you can face the error and argue it down you can cure the sick.'[10] This belief in turn led to the development of Christian Science, one of

America's largest new religious movements. Its founder, Mary Baker Eddy, was apparently one of Quimby's patients.

Homoeopathy and chiropractic may seem less 'alternative' than some other therapies – and certainly, both have been more widely accepted by the medical establishment. But they also emerged from the same mystical view, in which matter and spirit were perceived as part and parcel of one entity. Samuel Christian Hahnemann (1755–1843), founder of homoeopathy, described the workings of his theories as 'spirit-like'.[11] According to his biographer, he took his philosophical base from the eastern mysticism of Confucius, whom he described as 'the benefactor of humanity, who has shown us the straight path to wisdom and to God', and of whom he wrote in a letter shortly before he died, 'Soon I will embrace him in the kingdom of blissful spirits.'[12]

The father-and-son team of D. D. and B. J. Palmer, who developed chiropractic, similarly had no hesitation in placarding the metaphysical basis of their theories. Writing in 1910, the father put across a typically 'New Age' message when he claimed that

> Growth, unfoldment is seen everywhere. Each individualized portion of matter is but an epitome of the universe, each growing and developing toward a higher sphere of action. . . The Universal Intelligence collectively or individualized, desires to express itself in the best manner possible. . . Man's aspirations should be to advance to a superior level, to make himself better, physically, mentally, and spiritually.[13]

The son, B. J. Palmer, wrote a number of popular works (including one on reincarnation), all making a direct link between spiritual progress and chiropractic: 'Everything that man could ask or pray for he has within . . . The Chiropractor removes the obstruction, adjusts the cause, and there are going to be effects.'[14]

The same themes are commonplace in today's holistic health movement. The entry on 'Chiropractic' in *The Holistic Health Handbook* has this to say: 'the universe is perfectly organized and . . . as extensions of that universal intelligence, we also have an unlimited potential for life and health . . . In order to express more of your potential, you need only keep the channels of that expression open.'[15]

Though still in the field, chiropractic has been overtaken in popularity by other bodywork therapies such as Reiki and Rolfing. Health is regularly understood in terms of self-discovery, especially the awareness that we are all part of some spiritual entity that is far larger than ourselves. *The Holistic Health Handbook* again affirms that 'we are all affected by the universal Life Energy'.[16] Tuning into this energy is what alternative medicine is all about, whether the energy is manifested through physical force fields, the channeling of spirit guides, the magical powers of crystals or the concepts of eastern mysticism.

THERAPIES

It would be impossible to deal comprehensively here with the whole range of alternative medical care. There are hundreds of theories and techniques already in vogue – and new ones are being promoted all the time. But it will be helpful to single out one or two specific examples, to show how closely the general assumptions of holistic health relate to the New Age worldview.

If there is such a thing as a typical New Age healing technique, then colour therapy has got to be it. Every

New Age fair has its complement of holistic aura-readers, claiming to be able to see clairvoyantly the etheric electromagnetic colour fields that are supposed to surround every living thing. Depending on what they discover, they may prescribe various treatments in order to keep your personal light spectrum in balance. The thinking behind this is related to Alice Bailey's view (channeled from Tibetan Masters) that we all exist in four forms: the physical body, the etheric body, the astral body and the mental body. So far as healing is concerned, the etheric body is the key. This is comprised of pure energy, and as such never loses its health and vitality. In the words of Djwhal Khul, channeled through Bailey, its main purpose is to 'vitalize and energize the physical body and thus integrate it into the energy body of the Earth and of the solar system'.[17] If the energy of this etheric body is enabled to flow directly into the physical body, everything will come together.

Popular promotions of colour therapy frequently imply that it is all about helping you to choose what colour clothes to wear to match your hair or skin type, or indeed the seasons of the year. But the basic thinking behind it is heavily spiritual and metaphysical, not merely cosmetic, and stems directly from the belief that light is the major type of energy in the universe. It is generally claimed that everything is light. Even apparently dense objects such as brick walls, tables and chairs are really made of light – but light that is pulsating at such low frequency levels that we perceive it as being solid. On this understanding, we are all walking energy fields. But light is not a simple energy. Watch light shining through a prism, and you see the seven colours of the rainbow – colours, it is claimed, that are vitally important for human health and well-being. This is why the aura is supposed to cover the whole spectrum of light frequencies. For the seven basic colours correspond to the seven *chakras* or spiritual power centres of the body identified in much eastern mysticism (though some healers now claim to be able to identify twelve of them). These *chakras* are located along the spinal column, and each has a different colour associated with it. The correct flow of light through the *chakras* will ensure continuing vitality and power and will stimulate healing.

The proportions of the colours in our personal aura determine whether we are well or ill. If colours like grey or navy blue – or especially black – predominate, then that's bad news. The presence of bright colours like gold, blue, green or white shows that all is well. Wearing the colours that are not strongly represented can help to strengthen the aura. But the same effect can allegedly be achieved simply by visualizing the appropriate colours. Each one has power to induce higher vibrations in the consciousness, thereby healing various parts of the body. So white will produce a high state of spiritual attunement; silver will trigger off artistic and creative vibrations; yellow will enhance intelligence and inventiveness; orange brings joy and vitality; indigo helps control bleeding; lavender promotes sentimentality and nostalgia – and so on, through the whole spectrum. If you know what's wrong with you, you can put it right by tuning in to the appropriate colour.

This is all based on the familiar New Age view that the whole cosmos consists of just one divine essence or energy-force, common to people, the natural world and the world of spirit. Each plane of reality expresses the same energy, though at different vibrations. As John Keel puts it in his book *The Eighth Tower:* 'The standard definition of God, "God is light", is just a simple way of saying that God is energy. Electromagnetic energy. He is not a He but an It; a field of energy that permeates the entire universe.'[18]

The same outlook inspires the use of crystals for healing, though their place in alternative medicine goes back further than colour therapy. In modern times, they were popularized by Baron Charles von Reichanbach, a nineteenth-century disciple of Mesmer. Instead of using just the hands to control the flow of 'animal magnetism', he passed crystals over the bodies of his patients, especially quartz crystals, which he believed were particularly effective in freeing up the flow of force fields. Modern therapists utilize crystals to attune the *chakras* properly, identifying different crystals with different *chakras*. So, for example, amethyst at the forehead is supposed to improve clairvoyance, while lapis lazuli at the throat will improve communication skills. There is a whole hierarchy of crystals, each with its own particular purpose. Crystals are mostly used in their normal form as stones. But you can also buy crystal bowls which, it is claimed, will create vibrations that induce altered states of consciousness. It is even possible to have your teeth filled with crystals by holistic New Age dentists! Crystals may be used for the healing of specific conditions, but as with colours, the major focus of interest lies in their spiritual powers. As Korra Deaver says, 'crystal is able to tap the energies of the universe'.[19] Something that is claimed for magic charms the world over.

Of course, it is not essential to use anything other than one's own body to tap into these mystical forces. As with channeling, one of the great attractions of alternative medicine has always been that anyone can learn how to do it. Samuel Thomson, a nineteenth-century American healer, adopted the slogan, 'To make every man his physician'.[20] One of today's most popular do-it-yourself methods – widely adopted even by conventional medicine – is the technique of Therapeutic Touch. This idea comes from Dolores Kreiger, who uses the Hindu concept of *prana* to give identity to the store of cosmic metaphysical energy. In her best-selling book *The Therapeutic Touch*, she describes how would-be healers should first contact this energy by purifying their own *chakras*. After this they will be able to communicate it to others. So 'The act of healing . . . [entails] the channeling of this energy flow by the healer for the well-being of the sick individual'.[21]

This is not unlike Reiki, one of the favourite New Age bodywork therapies. It is described by Reiki Master Glenda Rye in the following terms:

> Reiki is the art and science of consistently being able to tap into the universal life force energy to promote spiritual, mental, and physical healing . . . The energy flows through the healer corresponding to the needs of the client. The healer also receives energy as it flows through them . . . There is no need to remove clothes. Reiki will go through clothes, blankets, and even casts. The desire to learn and the attunements are all you need. Spiritual growth and physical healing will be nurtured by the universe.

Though she goes on to claim that 'Reiki is not a religion, dogma, or cult', it – like Therapeutic Touch and all similar procedures – clearly promotes a distinctive religious viewpoint, namely that the same divine essence runs through people, plants and animals, and the cosmic world of spirit. R. C. Fuller has no hesitation in concluding that when conventional medicine uses these methods, it is 'not simply introducing nurses to new

techniques that will supplement the impersonal and
overly materialistic therapies associated with medical
science . . . [but is] promulgating a new world view in
which the physical is understood to be enveloped by a
metaphysical agent undetected by the senses'.[22]

HEALTH AND WHOLENESS

Health has always gone hand in hand with larger issues in
life, such as being happy and fulfilled. In his famous
hierarchy of needs, American sociologist Abraham
Maslow identified basic good health as one of the
foundations for any kind of satisfactory existence.
Without health, nothing else is possible, because being
unhealthy inevitably places severe restrictions on life's
possibilities. But what exactly is health? Is it a smoothly
functioning body? Or is it something more – wholeness of
personality?

Traditional medical science has gone for the first of
these definitions: people are basically bodies, made like
machines out of many different parts, and disease occurs
when the parts break down. Therefore, repairing the
parts – by drugs or surgery – will restore a person to
health. As the eminent nineteenth-century American
doctor Benjamin Rush put it, regular medical practice
proceeds on the basis of 'direct and drastic interferences'
with the biological systems of the patient. In his day, this
meant procedures like bloodletting, or dosing with
poisons such as mercury, arsenic, opium and strychnine –
or even, on occasion, branding with red-hot irons – in the
attempt to clear out the patient's system. Such practices
were mostly ineffective, and quite frequently fatal, and
modern medicine has rightly moved on from all that. But
'direct and drastic interferences' are still the basic

methodology. Electronic gadgets are being used more and more to keep people artificially 'alive' when all possible hope of restoration has long since disappeared. Sometimes this goes on for years at a time, and always at enormous cost to relatives who find themselves not only paying the doctors but also getting involved in complex litigation to try to have the life-support machines turned off. As the French philosopher Voltaire once said: 'Physicians pour drugs of which they know little, to cure diseases of which they know less, into humans of which they know nothing.'

Alternative medicine takes a different line. We all know that it is possible to have a perfect body and still be unhappy – or, conversely, to be physically disabled and yet personally fulfilled. Human happiness is much more than just the sum of its parts, and seems to be located somewhere in the interplay between different aspects of the human personality. Holistic medicine claims to be treating not merely sickness or disease, but the whole person – body, mind and spirit. This is why knowing who you are is of vital importance in New Age medicine – and why at the end of the day it almost always comes down to specifically religious or spiritual considerations. For in this context, self-awareness demands a cosmic consciousness of who we are, where we have come from, why we are here, and who we are becoming – all of which is invariably understood along the lines of the worldview discussed in the previous chapter. One practitioner described his craft to me as 'energy medicine, not chemical medicine'.

Alternative medicine redefines the conventional western understanding of health and healing. To the mainline medic, healing requires that a cure should take place. No cure means failure, and death is the ultimate failure. The radiologist with whom we began this chapter assumed that if death looked likely, then nothing else of value could happen, whereas the holistic healer will claim that, even if death is inevitable, healing can still take place. When a 1990 report written by conventional medical experts condemned the Cancer Help Centre at Bristol, England, as being ineffectual and a waste of money, the Centre defended itself by claiming that healing is not necessarily the same thing as continued living, and that disease is not something restricted to particular organs, but is symptomatic of a damaged person. If dying well is the same thing as being healthy, then clearly the rules of the game are being substantially rewritten. This is why Marilyn Ferguson can identify the rise and development of the hospice movement as being part of the New Age 'Aquarian Conspiracy'. For once we start to look at the relationships between mind, body and spirit – treating people in their entirety rather than just as collections of diseased organs – then healing can take place even where a person is facing death. As one AIDS sufferer put it to me, 'Confronting death can make your life better.'

New Age thinking often surfaces most clearly in preparation for death. Many death therapies now depend heavily on the channeling of spirit guides and on entering into altered states of consciousness as ways of helping people come to terms with their situation. Counsellors for the dying are encouraged to use past-life regression therapy as a means of enabling patients to understand what death is like. The reasoning behind this unlikely-sounding idea is simple: if we have all lived before, then we must all have died before. Mind, body and spirit are connected not just in this existence, but on the cosmic astral plane as well. The experience of death is therefore nothing new or unusual, and by reliving the deaths of the past we can prepare ourselves the more effectively for the end of this life when it comes.

EXPLANATIONS AND QUESTIONS

Most ordinary people have no idea what to make of all this. Scientific medicine typically dismisses even the apparent successes of alternative therapy as due to credulity, suggestion or even just coincidence – arguing that patients would have got better anyway, whether or not they had received these treatments. Unquestionably, there are many charlatans at work in holistic health care, who are exploiting vulnerable people suffering from life-threatening diseases, and offering in return only bizarre and sometimes painful treatments. It was no surprise to me when the person with whose story I began this chapter received a letter from a holistic practitioner, offering to relieve him of a large sum of money in the elusive search for a cure for his particular condition. Dr Karol Sikora, a cancer specialist at London's Hammersmith Hospital, describes the case of a thirty-nine-year-old woman who went to see him with a grotesque breast tumour in an advanced state. For a year she had avoided visiting a conventional medic, and instead had received injections of iscador, a homoeopathic mistletoe extract. 'Cancer doctors see this sort of thing again and again,' said Dr Sikora, commenting that with prompter action and more orthodox treatment this woman's life may well have been saved. He also added: 'My feeling is that it makes patients feel better. It doesn't actually cure cancer but it helps patients take chemotherapy and radiotherapy who couldn't take it before and would jack it in saying they'd had enough. If it helps you tolerate the treatment better, then it can "cure" the cancer."[23]

That sort of comment is significant. It can hardly be coincidence that just about every alternative treatment involves the laying on of hands. That alone makes it very different from conventional practice. But what does this physical contact actually accomplish? In particular, is it – as its practitioners claim – really about feeling energy flows, restoring balance and channeling cosmic forces into the human body? Or is it a form of personal affirmation that can have powerful results simply because many westerners are starved of physical contact? There are countless examples showing that a person's ability to survive a crisis increases dramatically with physically expressed support. Prisoners in concentration camps have been able to endure the most horrific atrocities as a result of love, companionship and affirmation. These things enhance our well-being. Cancer sufferers often have to put up with what is described as 'skin-hunger'. People stop touching them. This is not surprising, given the inhibitions that so many people have about physical contact, even with the healthy. Any touching will obviously have a very positive result for the sufferer. It is interesting in this connexion to note R. C. Fuller's conclusion that what happens in holistic medicine is similar to what in other times and places would have been rites of religious initiation. These therapies 'give to individuals for whom religion has consisted of dull habits and lifeless doctrines handed to them by others both experiences and concepts that turn it into a personally meaningful way of life'. Is this why the process of receiving such treatment is often more helpful for people than the actual therapeutic outcome? It certainly helps to explain why those involved in this scene can so readily accept ideas that are considerably at variance with either established science or established theology.

There are many features of holistic health that can only be assessed in relation to a careful analysis of their practical performance. But some aspects of this whole way of thinking do give real cause for concern. The New Age insistence that 'you choose to be who you are' surfaces in alternative medicine as the belief that 'you choose your own state of health'. Up to a point, you do, of course. If you stick with a diet heavy in fatty foods and red meat, smoke a hundred cigarettes a day, drink a lot of alcohol and never take any exercise, then sooner or later you're likely to have life-threatening problems. But this simple pattern of cause and effect is not what is generally in view. For choosing your own health is frequently related to wider cosmic choices made in a spiritual existence before this one. After all, if you choose when to be born and who to be, you presumably also choose how and when you're going to die. You may also choose to suffer from certain illnesses, either consciously because you wish to learn whatever spiritual lessons are to be discovered therein, or unconsciously because you have lost touch with your Higher Self or spirit guides. According to J. L. Simmons, 'Deeply woven karmic habit patterns may keep us chronically ill, or on a terminal disease course. . . We may have planned to undergo such an experience in this lifetime to learn from it'.[24] Caroline Myss, whose speciality is intuitive diagnosis, believes that people's attitudes actually create different illnesses. So for example, 'marked lack of trust is a very significant factor in the creation of a stroke', while 'All forms of arthritis are created in response to feelings of irritation, frustration and anger.'[25] In the same collection of writings, Louise L. Hay identifies everything from AIDS to acne as having a self-determined cause. While cancer therapist Carl Simonton draws the obvious conclusion that 'If we are going to believe that we have the power in our own bodies to overcome cancer, then we have to admit that we also had the power to bring on the disease in the first place.' Something with which J. L. Simmons clearly agrees: 'a being will decide to terminate its incarnation in a particular physical life form when the quality of life is no longer suitable for its purpose'.[26] Even Marilyn Ferguson, who is one of the more perceptive and morally sensitive New Age thinkers, asserts unhesitatingly that 'All illness, whether cancer or schizophrenia or a cold, originates in the bodymind.' Cancer, for example, seems to be prevalent in people who 'tend to keep their feelings to themselves, and most have not had close relationships with their parents. They find it difficult to express anger. . . they are conforming and controlled, less autonomous and spontaneous than those whose tests later prove negative.'[27]

All I can say is, try comforting a cancer patient with that. Can it ever be so simple? Lesley Fallowfield, a psychologist with the British-based Cancer Research Campaign, makes this perceptive comment: 'There is a feeling that if you eat a proper diet or change your personality characteristics the cancer will probably regress. This is fine for some people but I've met patients who not only had to cope with the problem of recurrent disease, but also with the guilt that they'd allowed this to happen by not following the programme.'[28] Just as the New Age worldview gives no hope to those who are economically marginalized and oppressed, it also offers no comfort to those who are suffering. Can any outlook that abandons belief in the existence of undeserved evil ever say anything worthwhile to the vast majority of the world's people? A world in which there are no victims is not the world as most of us know and experience it. It is not the world as it truly is.

QUESTIONS FOR CHRISTIANS

As with everything else related to the New Age, it is impossible to generalize here. Not all alternative practitioners would agree that we choose to be ill. Some have claimed that they are merely rediscovering techniques that in reality go back to Jesus Himself. In his popular volume *The Bigness of the Fellow Within*, chiropractor B. J. Palmer claimed that Jesus healed people by channeling energy from the cosmic source that he called the Innate. A similar claim is also made by Ambrose and Olga Worrall in their book *The Miracle Healers* – though they also allege that he, like them, was diagnosing and treating illness by means of channeled messages received from spirit guides and extraterrestrials.[29] Bizarre claims of this sort are matched on the Christian side by equally weird notions that if you go to an acupuncturist or a yoga class – or keep a few crystals in your home – you may well find yourself possessed by demons as a result. For there is increasing hostility towards alternative treatments in certain sections of the Church. The worldview of much, if not all, alternative medicine is New Age, it is claimed; such medicine should therefore be avoided like the plague. Christians should stick to conventional scientific medicine instead.

This is a curious proposition. There is no doubt that, both in terms of historical origins and its own internal logic, alternative medicine is not easily compatible with a Christian worldview – and Christians who regularly use

such therapies frequently play this down quite unjusti-
fiably. But those who suggest that going to a conventional
doctor, and trusting modern medical science is the
'Christian' thing to do are conveniently ignoring the fact
that conventional medicine is also based on a worldview
that is fundamentally opposed to the Christian outlook.
As in so many other things, Christians have undermined
their own integrity with the easy assumption that
Christian values are identical with the values of modern
western culture. The reality is that the scientific
materialist basis of conventional medicine is neither
more nor less Christian than the monistic worldview of
alternative therapists. Indeed in some respects a rationalist view is, if anything, the more anti-Christian of the
two, inasmuch as it consistently denies that there is
anything that might be labelled a spiritual dimension to
the human personality, and insists that the body is
a totally self-contained and independent mechanical
system. At least the New Age outlook affirms that people
have a spiritual dimension, however muddled and
mistaken the New Age concept of that spirit might be.

There is a pressing need here for someone to work out
what a truly Christian view of health might look like.
Until they do, Christians should be pragmatists. The fact
is that both systems of health care do seem to work, at
least some of the time. It would be foolish to deny
that many advances have come about as a result of
conventional medical science. The same could be said of
alternative medicine. In particular, both the holistic
emphasis that we are more than merely bodies, and
the corresponding concern for the interplay of mind,
body and spirit, are thoroughly Christian values. The
importance of personal affirmation and the need for
inner healing were emphasized by Jesus himself.

Painful memories and guilt will never be healed by drugs. Most of the healing process needs to take place inside – and Jesus, who knew what was in people, recognized this and acted upon it.

Despite the last 200 years of scientific progress, there are still many things we do not understand about the human body and its workings, and Christians must gladly accept any new knowledge as a part of the God-given miracle of life itself. That is not the same thing as naive acceptance of the latest fads and fashions, whether they be 'scientific' or otherwise. The energy fields of which alternative therapists talk may or may not exist. Their treatments may or may not work. And if they do work, they may not do so for the reasons they think they do. Medical treatment of any sort is not necessarily and directly religious, though I am quite certain that most holistic practitioners either play down or deliberately conceal the spiritual suppositions on which they operate. At the end of the day, though, Australian author John Harris is right when he argues that medical therapies 'only become manifestations of the New Age when they are seen to be regulated by some form of mystical, spiritual energy, or when they are adhered to because of a belief in reincarnation or pantheism'.[30] Remember that Jesus claimed to be the 'truth'. If he is, that means any truth found either in scientific or alternative medicine must somehow be related to him. To believe otherwise would be to deny some central Christian convictions.

HEALING THE EARTH

J. L. Simmons calls the environmental movement 'a first cousin to the spiritual awakening movement',[31] and with only very slight changes in terminology, much of what we have said about holistic health could also be said of the environment. Indeed, some writers make direct connexions between personal health and well-being and the state of the planet. As long ago as 1852, an anonymous editorial in the *Watercure Journal* claimed that 'The natural state of man, as of all plants and animals, is one of uninterrupted health. . . '[32] Acupuncturist Mark Duke also sees cosmic significance in his own treatments: 'The acupuncturist. . . brings his patients back to health not only for their own sake and happiness, but so that the whole world may function properly. Every needle the acupuncturist twirls between his fingers bears the heavy weight of universal harmony in its slim, pointed end.'[33]

The same sort of idea – that we can actually influence not only who we are, but the nature of reality itself – inspired the Harmonic Convergence back in 1987. Just as people are now searching for personal wholeness, bringing together mind, body and spirit, so in world terms many are looking to find the interconnectedness of the physical universe. Far from being the impersonal machine that western science has conventionally assumed, the earth is alive and has energies of its own. Energies that some claim can be traced and measured. Dowsing, pendulums and other techniques are used to do this, and 'energy maps' are produced, based on the location of such things as 'ley lines', corn circles and ancient standing stones. These are the energies that alternative medics often speak of, and some New Agers do not hesitate to give them personal characteristics – I once heard them described as 'the veins and arteries of the earth's nervous system'. The idea that the earth itself is somehow alive received unexpected backing from the scientist James E. Lovelock's 1979 book, *Gaia: a new look at life on earth*. Not only did he argue that the earth is one interlocking symbiotic system, with people as just a part of it, but he also introduced the term 'Gaia' into the New Age vocabulary. Whether intentionally or not, he thereby gave the environmental movement a spiritual dimension. For Gaia was the name of the Earth Mother goddess in ancient Greek mythology.

Some want to understand all this in the most literal form imaginable. If the whole world of nature has a life of its own, perhaps the ancient Greeks got it right. Dorothy Maclean, one of the founders of the Findhorn Community, certainly thought so. In a message from spirit guides received in 1963, she was told to 'co-operate in the garden by thinking about the Nature Spirits . . . the Spirits of different physical forms, such as the spirits of the clouds, of rain, of the separate vegetables. In the new world their realm will be quite open to humans – or, should I say, humans will be quite open to them.'[34] Just how open was subsequently revealed by Robert Ogilvie Crombie, who in 1966 claimed to have met the Greek god Pan in the garden at Findhorn. After a conversation with Pan he was instructed to preserve a wild area there for the benefit of these nature spirits.

Not all New Agers go that far. But many are trying to rediscover the divine nature of the earth, and usually they talk of an earth goddess. It has come to be an unquestioned assumption that picturing God as masculine is a root cause of environmental destruction, and that nature is essentially feminine in character. Connect that to the view that male ways of looking at things allegedly lead to fragmentation and confrontation, and that the female principle homes in on wholeness and harmony instead, and you have a very strong challenge to traditional western patriarchal religion, Christianity in particular. Terence McKenna, a New Age leader from

Sonoma County, California, puts it succinctly if brutally: 'The Judeo-Christian ethic is that man is the lord of creation, and can do as he wishes. The pagan, archaic-revival point of view is biological, ecological, and stresses co-adaptive relations. We are in a global suicidal crisis – and Christianity has a lot to answer for.'[35]

Large numbers of environmental activists take the same position. But the idea that Christians are to blame for the mess the world is in is, at best, naive and uninformed. Quite often, it is deliberately malicious. The Baltic Sea is at least as polluted as the Mediterranean – and that has happened as a direct result of the worldview of atheistic communism, one of the most fiercely anti-Christian systems the world has ever seen. Moreover, the track record of eastern cultures, based on a supposedly holistic worldview that acknowledges a spiritual harmony between people and the forces of nature, is just the same. Thailand's tropical rain forests were being systematically destroyed at an alarming rate for almost half a century before anything at all started to happen in Brazil – again by the devotees of a so-called 'holistic' religion. Japan – with a very similar traditional worldview – is the one country in the world that allows the routine slaughter of whales and dolphins. By all means at the same time look back into the pages of European history and observe that the leaders in the Industrial Revolution were mostly Christians, who sometimes exploited both their own workers and the wider environment in the constant search for financial reward. No one could deny that Christians have played their part in messing up the environment. But on all the available evidence, no one could conclude that environmental pollution is somehow a natural outcome of Christianity. People of all religions, and also those with no religion, have done their share. We have all treated the natural world as just the raw material for technological progress, in the process reducing it to a collection of spare parts for our own consumption. The problem is not related to religious systems: it is deeply ingrained in the human disposition, and we are all guilty.

To people with a New Age worldview, the most obvious way to reverence our world again is to recognize its innate divinity. For anyone who believes that they, God and everything else in the universe are all one, this makes sense – and if evidence of apparently invisible energy fields can be brought in to back this view up, so much the better. Of course, the evidence of energy fields does no such thing. Assuming they exist, and that phenomena such as corn circles and standing stones can reasonably be explained on this basis, the existence of energy fields is neither more nor less than the existence of energy fields. It is a big jump from there to proving that this is some kind of psychic or spiritual energy. And a further enormous leap of imagination is required to get from there to the belief that the world is a divine entity. The fact that the world is a series of interlocking systems and can best be understood in terms of coherence and interconnectedness is compatible with a whole variety of religious explanations, of which monism is just one. It is equally compatible with the opinion that the Creator made things this way. But neither of these religious explanations is actually demanded by the facts.

Many environmental activists are attracted to the idea that people are a part of the natural process, and that therefore we will put things right by getting in tune with the cosmos and doing what comes naturally. But some New Agers have hesitations about this, for it conflicts with other central aspects of the New Age spiritual search, especially the concern with self-discovery and inner human development. Writing in *Gnosis* magazine, Richard Smoley identifies this incongruity and wants to distance himself from it: 'There is a danger, I believe, in equating God with nature. . . man is not fundamentally of nature. The truest, deepest part of him is beyond the cycle of reproduction and survival. To deify nature is to forget this and to put man at the mercy of this cycle rather than to help him transcend it'.[36]

There is also another problem here. New Age environmentalists often speak glibly about living in harmony with nature, being your own truth, living your own truth, and so on, and take it for granted that doing this will automatically promote harmony, peace and stability in the future, and may even reverse some of the damage of the past. But such naive propositions can only seem sensible if we refuse to face the facts of the past. For doing what comes naturally has been the cause of the problem. It is precisely because we have lived for generations by our own private truth values that we have got things into such a mess to start with. It has been the act of choosing for ourselves, without regard either for the welfare of others or for the cosmic consequences, that has led to such widespread devastation of the planet. To imagine that we can get out of the mess we have created by redefining this self-centredness, elevating it to a virtue and calling it 'God' – or 'Goddess' – is naive and unrealistic. The philosophy of doing what comes naturally leads directly to the conclusion that ultimately no one is responsible for their own actions. To observe that we have created our own living hell by making choices that suit our own interests is not narrow-minded dogmatism: it is simply stating an obvious fact. Once more, the weak spot of the whole New Age outlook proves to be its inability to cope with the sheer brutal facts of human life. Whether we like it or not, human evil is a fact, and we cannot make it go away just by denying its existence, or redefining it in some fancy psychological or environmental jargon. Exploitation – whether of the environment or other people – is real, and at the end of the day the basic issues are not metaphysical or psychological: they are moral. The problem is not the way people are, but the way they choose to behave.

New Agers are good at asking the right questions. Their answers are less satisfactory. In the area of health and the environment, however, Christians apparently have little to offer as a distinctive alternative. Concern for the environment should certainly be a Christian priority. But what would a Christian ecological perspective look like? The raw materials are there from which such a viewpoint can be fashioned. They are to be found in a striking form in a most unexpected place – the teaching of Paul. He had no doubt that if the Christian Gospel was indeed to be 'good news', then it had to provide salvation not only for individuals, but also for the whole world system (Colossians 1:15–20, Romans 8:18–25). Unlike the New Age outlook, the New Testament takes seriously the reality of evil, and that fact alone should give Christians a head start. But there is much work to be done to translate it all into a practical environmental policy that can be applied to the circumstances of our own day.

Chapter 6

GETTING IT ALL TOGETHER

*T*HE training of top executives by multinational corporations may seem to be an unlikely place to uncover the influence of the New Age Movement. At first glance, the world of big business looks to be light years removed from some of the concerns documented in previous chapters. Esoteric healing techniques, mystical contacts with extraterrestrial spirit guides and the development of cosmic consciousness seem to have little in common with the aims and objectives of the market-place – except in so far as a few successful entrepreneurs have made themselves rich by purveying the paraphernalia required to follow through such concerns.

But the reality is quite different. The last fifteen years have seen management consultants adopt New Age methodologies on a grand scale, and more controversy has been generated by the use of these techniques than by any other single issue involving values and morality in the corporate workplace. The subject began to hit the headlines in a big way in 1987, when the US Public Utilities Commission found it necessary to censure Pacific Bell for a training course known as 'Kroning' – a programme which was not only horrifically expensive but which some participants alleged to be manipulative and threatening. By the end of the following year, the level of public concern in the USA was so great that the Equal Employment Opportunities Commission was forced to publish a special series of guidelines advising employers how to handle training courses that have frequently led to complex legal cases. Usually these cases involve the allegation that the courses violate either the Constitution or the Civil Rights Act, which protects workers from discrimination based on religion, race, sex, age and ethnic background.

So what happens at a New Age management course? I've already related one true story in the first chapter of this book. Admittedly, that was a fairly extreme example, and not all New Age training courses would take the same form. But the experience already described there, while not universal, is sufficiently widespread to give rise to genuine concern about the techniques and procedures used by some of these trainers. That particular course raised questions at many different levels. The most obvious bone of contention was the fact that the company infringed the workers' personal freedom by taking them off to an unknown destination and dumping them in the middle of nowhere then throwing them into a survival course for which they had been given no prior warning or preparation.

There is, of course, nothing wrong with pushing yourself to the physical and psychological limits as a means of identifyng personal strengths and weaknesses. In fact, such techniques are the stock-in-trade for the training of military personnel all over the world. It is not surprising that they – along with martial arts and other physical exercises – should have surfaced in training courses for people involved in the battlefield that is

corporate management. But there is a subtle difference
between army training and the way business trainers often
use such techniques. When you join the army, you expect
that sort of thing. When you report at your workplace for a
management course, kitted out only in a standard business
suit, you do not. Many people have no hesitation in using
terms like 'brainwashing' to describe that kind of pressure
and potential humiliation. It is bad enough to be
deliberately disorientated and manipulated in this way.
But when participants in such courses are informed (as
they invariably are) that their failure to see the nature of
their predicament more clearly is related to some kind of
mental blindness that can be corrected by a personal
spiritual realignment, then the scene is all set for confrontation. A difficult physical challenge is one thing, but
to invite people to abandon their regular worldview and
values for something else is a different matter altogether.

CONTROVERSIAL COURSES

I came across all this at first hand a couple of years ago.
Returning from a holiday in Tenerife, one of the first
places I headed for was my answerphone machine,
curious to know who had been trying to contact me in my
absence. As always, much of the tape was taken up with
people who called but chose not to leave a message. And
the rest of the messages were mostly ones I could have
done without. But there was one caller whose enigmatic
communication was as intriguing as it was unexpected. It
was from someone I'd never heard of before, who simply
said he had been fired from his job as a result of a New
Age management course, and he would like to meet me to
talk about it. At the time, I wondered what kind of
joker he might be, but I was sufficiently curious to

follow it up. And the story behind it was a real shocker.

The person in question was a Scottish electronics worker named Paul Mansbacher. Born in Zimbabwe, he was a committed Christian, and had carved out a highly successful career for himself as a computer systems manager. In late February 1989, he had been sent along with his colleagues to the French city of Nice for a regular training course called 'Improving Organization Effectiveness'. Nothing particularly unusual or threatening about that, you may think. Many British executives would just love to spend a week in a warmer climate at that time of year – and who doesn't want to be more effective? But within two months, and as a direct result of that course, Mansbacher had lost his job. His employer, a multinational computer corporation, later described it as a 'performance-related dismissal' – and offered to pay for a course of psychiatric treatment to modify his behaviour! But Mansbacher believed this was nothing but a smoke-screen for religious persecution, because the view which had been put across in the course had conflicted seriously with his own Christian convictions.

When I met him, it was immediately obvious that he held some very strong beliefs, and was not afraid to use strident language to express them. He had no hesitation in using words like 'blasphemous', 'satanic', and 'demonic' to describe his former employer's training materials, and he was equally forthright in his opinion of those who had taught the course that had led to his dismissal. I don't mind admitting that his attitude seemed so intemperate and, at times, almost fanatical that my natural instinct was to adopt a somewhat cynical attitude to some of his claims. But I was still interested, and when his story was picked up by the secular Scottish press, I decided it was worth a second look. I was absolutely staggered by what I discovered.

The course in question was largely based on materials emanating from the Seattle-based Pacific Institute, a business training organization headed up by self-made millionaire Lou Tice. I knew there had been a number of legal battles in the US courts over the methodology used in these courses, and though this group now claims it has nothing to do with the New Age Movement, it is a matter of simple fact that one of its most popular courses – 'Investment in Excellence' – was originally titled 'New Age Thinking'. Many of the techniques being promoted are designed to encourage participants to search for precisely the kind of personal paradigm shifts that are so characteristic of the mainstream New Age Movement. A 1989 news report quotes Tice himself as claiming: 'You have the power to become the Wizard of Oz. My affirmations are continually that I am a very powerful wizard . . . I bestow upon you the brains and habits to make yourself a better human being.' This message is reinforced, one way or another, in the twenty-four videos watched over four days that are an integral part of the courses.

Though he had questions about some of this, Tice was not the main problem for Mansbacher. That accolade was reserved for a book which had been used in the course – actually, a widely used and highly respected book by consultant Russell Ackoff, called *Creating the Corporate Future*. It was this academic text that was to prove the toughest challenge to Mansbacher's own personal religious beliefs. To see just exactly what all the fuss was about, I decided I would have to read it for myself. Once you get past the first three chapters, there is a wealth of invaluable expertise relating to the creation of interactive management systems. But the introductory section, which sets out the ideological and philosophical background to it all, is heavily laced with mystical and spiritual concepts – and is undoubtedly controversial. To put it simply, the author surveys western culture over the last two or three centuries, and concludes that Christian values are largely to blame for the mess in which industry often finds itself. Confrontation between workers and managers, the alienation of the workforce, the dehumanizing attitudes which regard people as expendable cogs in a machine – all these and many other negative features are, he claims, simply the natural outcome of the Christian view of God.

This argument is based on a social and historical analysis that no one could reasonably quarrel with. Ackoff points out that since the Second World War the West has been in a period of profound change – change of such speed and significance that we today are at a great crossroads in history. One age is coming to an end, and a 'new age' (no capital letters) is beginning. The intermediate stage, where we are now, is an unsettling time of upheaval, and this disturbance will continue until the new age has finally arrived. In this interim period, 'both our methods of understanding the world and our actual understanding of it are undergoing fundamental and profound transformations'. Today's generation therefore stands at a unique point in history, as heirs to the past but masters of the future: '. . .the problems it confronts are inherited, but those of us who intend to have a hand in shaping the new age are trying to face them in a new way'[1]

Ackoff often refers to the 'new age' and much of what he says is so obvious it hardly needs to be reiterated. But all this talk of a new age dawning is certainly not inconsistent with the populist and more apocalyptic style of New Age vision, with its expectation of some kind of messiah figure who will usher in a new world order – especially when Ackoff uses so much mystical imagery to define the precise form of this coming 'new age':

> The Systems Age is a movement of many wills in which each has only a small part to play . . . It is taking shape before our eyes. It is still too early, however, to foresee all the difficulties that it will generate. Nevertheless, I believe the new age can be trusted to deal with them. Meanwhile there is much work to be done, much scope for greater vision, and much room for enthusiasm and optimism.[2]

It all sounds very much like a more intellectual version of the kind of media hype that has surrounded the Harmonic Convergence and similar events.

In business-speak, the old age we are leaving is described as the 'Machine Age', while the new age that is in the process of coming to birth is the 'Systems Age'. The terminology has a long and honourable history. It goes back to Ludwig von Bertalanffy, a German biologist who promoted a science of context called 'perspectivism', which laid the foundations for what subsequently came to be known as General Systems Theory. Put simply, this states that nothing can fully be understood in isolation, but will only make sense within its total context, or 'system'. Each component in any system interacts with all the other components in such a way that it is both impossible and pointless to try to separate them.

Concepts of this sort have shed new light on many areas of modern understanding. The environmental movement, for example, is based on the fact that the natural ecological system of which we are all a part is much bigger and more complex than the various constituent elements that go to make it up. Another example is modern science. It is undoubtedly a far cry from the classical rationalist doctrine popularized during the optimistic days of the European Enlightenment. Then it was taken for granted that the only way to understand anything – from literature to anatomy – was to take it apart to identify its basic ingredients. Only then – if anything was left – would it be permissible to try to put it all back together again. Inflexible concepts of cause and effect were used to analyze everything, and a virtue was made of keeping things separate – even to the extent of constructing an artificial context for experimentation (the laboratory), where by definition the influence of the natural environment was excluded. Little wonder, then, that western culture for the last two centuries has been largely fragmented and has lacked a holistic vision.

The evidence of such fragmentation is plain for all to see. Many of the institutions of western culture – political, religious, industrial, educational – are bureaucratic and impersonal, operating within rigid mechanistic frameworks that at best lead to fragmentation and conformity, and at worst actually deny some of our most cherished ideals. Though knowledge of it has scarcely begun to trickle through to the average person, modern science recognized the inadequacy of all this several decades ago, and has all but abandoned the old reductionist approach for a new, holistic understanding.

This growing recognition that things can only be fully understood in their context has marked a major step forward – in the physical sciences, in medicine, and in the workplace. Could it possibly be that the problems of modern industrial structures are related to the acceptance of artificial boundaries between workers and managers, and that the relative inefficiency of both is related to the way their work-life has been isolated from their overall lifestyle and values? If taking things apart is the cause of our difficulties, then it follows that putting them together will bring new insights.

BELIEFS AND SYSTEMS

So far, so good. These are all important and perfectly legitimate questions. Nor is it anti-religious to ask them. In the last decade a whole multiplicity of church growth courses based on exactly the same kind of thinking has been eagerly embraced within mainstream western Christianity! But when Ackoff begins to explain the reasons behind all this fragmentation and disharmony, some unexpected and (for the Christian) unwelcome dimensions begin to creep into his analysis. The bad old Machine Age, he claims, was characterized by two basic beliefs: 'that the universe was a machine created by God to do His work, and that He had created man in his image'. This in turn produced the conclusion that 'man ought to be creating machines to do his work' – a belief that led quite naturally and inevitably to the philosophy of the Inudstrial Revolution, which Ackoff describes as

a consequence of man's efforts to imitate God by creating machines to do his work. The industrial organizations produced . . . were taken to be related to their creators, their owners, much as the universe was to God . . . employees were treated as replaceable machines or machine parts even though they were known to be human beings. Their personal objectives, however, were considered irrelevant by employers . . . the very simple repetitive tasks they were given to do were designed as though they were to be performed by machines.[3]

In the process, both workers and managers were dehumanized. Their personal and family lives disintegrated in the face of the corporate machine and its many demands. And it was all the fault of western Christianity!

If the Machine Age was just Christianity projected into the corporate workplace, what kind of religious beliefs inspire and motivate the Systems Age? Though he gives a nod in the direction of freedom of choice for the individual worker, Ackoff leaves little room for doubt as to his own personal answer to that question: 'many individuals find comfort in assuming the existence of such a unifying whole' – and they can call it 'God'.

This God however, is very different from the Machine-Age God who was conceptualized as an individual who had created the universe. God-as-the-whole cannot be individualized or personified, and cannot be thought of as the creator. To do so would make no more sense than to speak of man as creator of his organs. In this holistic view of things man is taken as a part of God just as his heart is taken as a part of man.[4]

The openly non-Christian orientation of this view is crystal clear in what follows:

this holistic concept of God is precisely the one embraced by many Eastern religions which conceptualize God as a system, not as an element . . . There is some hope, therefore, that in the creation of systems sciences the culture of the East and West can be synthesized. The twain may yet meet in the Systems Age.[5]

It is not surprising that a man like Paul Mansbacher, with strong Christian beliefs, should have found all this hard to swallow. To him, the whole training course was pushing ideas that ran directly contrary to his own religious convictions. 'In one discussion they argued the case for us creating a new personality for God', he commented. 'They said the God of the old Machine Age was the Creator, and was an individual you could get to know. They then said that notion was history. In the Systems Age, they said, God is seen as an all-containing system of which we are all parts. He isn't a creator because he can't create. Then they said that concept of God could be found in some eastern religions.'

Anyone who has read this far will have little difficulty in identifying here a number of the key concepts that go to make up a typical New Age worldview. As such, New Agers have as much right as anyone else to make their views known. But when all this is being presented by business trainers as if it were objective facts, and managers are being compelled to attend courses which present it as such, can anyone really be surprised when religious believers find themselves compromised and affronted? Can you imagine the uproar there would be if the boot were on the other foot, and secular managers were being told by fundamentalist Christians that they need to be 'born again'? What has happened here to the much-vaunted pluralism of the modern western world, in which everyone is free to make their own choices? Could it possibly be that the only belief system people are not free to choose is mainstream orthodox Christianity? No doubt the answers to those questions are not exactly simple and clear-cut. But in the context of the corporate workplace, only the most naive personnel director would be unable to foresee that the introduction of such New

Age views into compulsory training courses would be bound to lead to legal action alleging the infringement of personal religious freedoms.

It is surprising how easily – and how often – textbooks on management skills blame the problems of western industry on what are perceived to be the religious attitudes of both workers and managers. But does it all stand up to critical scrutiny? Is it either true or fair to castigate the Church as the major cause of our society's problems? Or is this just another example of that buck-passing mentality so prevalent throughout industry, that is itself part of the problem we now face?

As a matter of fact, when we take a closer look, this perspective on western culture is nothing like as convincing as it might seem at first glance. No one would dispute that the mindset which we have inherited from the Industrial Revolution – despite all its achievements – has many built-in weaknesses, not least the dehumanizing of work and workers which Ackoff so eloquently identifies. But it is something else altogether to demonstrate that this is the logical outcome of the Christian belief in God as Creator.

For a start, is it really true that religion as such has ever exercised much influence at all in the organization of the typical industrial workplace? The drawing of easy connexions between religious views of God as a celestial machine-minder and the philosophy of modern managers is itself a good example of the blinkered sort of thinking that characterized the so-called Machine Age. Connexions like this can seem to make sense when you are sitting in an academic study isolated from the broader concerns of real life, but they hardly ever happen in the larger context of ordinary daily experience. The fact is that most modern managers are far too busy with other things to sit around speculating about such esoteric concerns. And the idea that the barons of the Industrial Revolution scoured books of theology looking for models of God as a way of improving efficiency and profits is just ludicrous. Nor did most of them make a study of Christian theology in their spare time. Nor did the majority of them even attend church, or actually claim to be Christian in any committed sense of the word.

Though we should not forget that some did. In Britain, two of the biggest confectionery empires were built up by people with strong Christian convictions – the Cadburys and the Rowntrees – and there can be no doubt that their 'model' factories were consciously founded on their view of God and of Christian principles. So if Ackoff's analysis is correct, we would expect them to provide us with examples of the worst excesses of manipulation and exploitation of the workers. Why is it then that their company structures – far from conforming to the stereotypes of the so-called Machine Age – actually reflected many of the more enlightened concepts now being advocated by systems theorists? The caring working communities which they created can readily be criticized for being too paternalistic, but the very existence of Christian industrialists with any sort of concern for workers as people puts a serious question mark against the simplistic assumption that Christianity is the root cause of the fragmentation and disharmony which now besets western culture.

In point of fact, the opening pages of the Bible itself speak of people as being 'in God's image' – a statement which, if taken seriously, hardly leads to the conclusion that workers can be indiscriminately exploited. Quite the reverse. Surely it implies that people are special, and need to be handled with consideration and care. If we really must find religious roots for everything, then it is far more likely that the exploitation and alienation of workers can be traced back to the rationalist and non-supernatural forms of religion that undermined the original Christian vision in the course of the Enlightenment, and which themselves were a direct product of the larger intellectual and social forces which also shaped European industrialization.

HOLISTIC SYSTEMS AND CHRISTIANITY

Systems thinking is not actually incompatible with the Christian Gospel, and it baffles me why management trainers should constantly blame 'Christianity' for the ailments of western culture. I can only conclude that they are either bigoted, or have some ulterior motive for putting Christians down. Or maybe they have such an inaccurate and half-baked understanding of what Christianity is about that they have no satisfactory basis on which to make any sort of sensible judgement.

As a matter of fact, the key documents of the Christian faith present their own distinctive models for the holistic environment in which women and men can achieve optimum maturity and self-fulfilment. A holistic viewpoint that even includes the physical environment, for the New Testament specifically states that new meaning in life will be found 'when the time is right . . . to bring all creation together' (Ephesians 1:10). Moreover, it spells out in some considerable detail what human relationships should look like in this holistic view of things. Saint Paul, for example, writes of the social, racial and gender barriers being dismantled, 'so there is no difference between Jews and Gentiles, between slaves and free people, between men and women. . .' (Galatians 3:28).

And in other passages, he describes the nature of the ideal framework within which such renewed human relationships can find their deepest fulfilment. In his characterization of the church as 'the body of Christ', we have one of the most profound descriptions of systems thinking anywhere in literature (1 Corinthians 12). Of course, he uses imagery and concepts that were no doubt more familiar to the people of his own day than they are to us. Comparing the ideal society to a body had a long history in Greek politics and philosophy well before Paul came on the scene. And the way he uses the comparison is unashamedly based on ancient notions of human physiology. But his meaning is unmistakable. In the ideal organizational structure, he claims, everyone is indispensable. No matter who they are, each person has a uniquely valuable role to play: 'The Spirit's presence is shown in some way in each person for the good of all.' Moreover, each person can be allowed to be himself or herself. They are all different – and that is not a weakness, but a strength: 'There are different kinds of spiritual gifts . . . different ways of serving . . . different abilities to perform service . . .' Yet they are all of equal value: 'All of you are Christ's body, and each one is a part of it'. What's more, everyone has a sense of responsibility. They know that they are inextricably linked with one another: 'If one part of the body suffers, all the other parts suffer with it; if one part is praised, all the other parts share its happiness.'

Ackoff highlights 'participative planning' as the management system for the new generation – a process which he describes as 'encouraging and facilitating the participation of the others in the design of and planning for the organizations and institutions of which they are a part'. Unless he has some hidden agenda, I would suggest that this biblical picture of the sort of organization which most truly reflects the character of the Christian God must be one of the most striking examples of what he is advocating. It is certainly exceedingly difficult, if not impossible, to reconcile what the Bible actually promotes with the negative and destructive stereotypes of Christianity that are all too easily accepted. Of course, western Christians have not always lived up to this ideal, any more than industrial managers always reach their targets – and we will have a lot more to say about this in our final chapter. But in assessing the practical performance of Christianity, we need to remember that the vast majority of the world's Christians are not in any case westerners. Well over half of them are not white, and the great growth centres of the world church are in the countries of Africa, South America and south-east Asia, not in the traditional heartlands of western Europe or North America. It is no coincidence that the amazing and well-documented growth of the Church in these other parts of the world is directly related to their rediscovery of the people-power of interactive organizations – only they call them 'base Christian communities', and take their inspiration not from systems analysis but from careful reading of the Bible.

It is in this light that we should also scrutinize New Age claims that a holistic lifestyle requires the backing of a mystical belief system in which some sort of divine essence or life-force runs through everything. Business people are always telling us that the only question that really interests them is whether a thing works. Forget the philosophical and academic hair-splitting, they say, and look at the practical results. So let's put this theory to the test of practical performance. It is a fact that all round the developing world today, the rediscovery of the Bible and the growth of the Church has become one of the leading catalysts for political and social improvement in the lives of millions of people. By contrast, consider the sort of society that the eastern mysticism advocated by New Agers has produced. As an example let's take the Indian sub-continent, where a so-called 'holistic' worldview has been dominant for centuries. Its most striking social product is the caste system – one of the most divisive, confrontational, fragmenting and personally degrading organizational structures imaginable. And it is so deeply engrained in the whole worldview that when in late 1990 the Indian government sought merely to mitigate its worst effects, without actually abolishing it, the result was the collapse of that government. How much room is there here for facilitating the kind of personal development that management trainers rate so highly? The question hardly needs to be given an answer. Even a cursory acquaintance with it all highlights the far-reaching inner inconsistency between the philosophical and religious foundation of what New Agers propose, and the proven practical outcome of it. We can agree with Ackoff when he writes that our aspirations for the future will be 'based on important and fundamental beliefs, attitudes, and commitments',[6] and that 'we cannot cope effectively with change unless we develop a better view of the world'.[7] But the proposed solution is hopelessly inadequate. The idea that western business people will somehow bring fulfilment and meaning into their own lives and those of others by adopting belief in 'God-as-the-whole' would have a decidedly hollow ring to the untouchables in the slums of Calcutta.

PERSONAL MANAGEMENT

But why are the untouchables there in the first place? Or, to broaden the question, why are so many people at the bottom of the pile, marginalized and unable to achieve their full potential as human beings? Why have blacks been so comprehensively abused in South Africa over much of this century? Why were so many innocent Jews and Gypsies callously put to death by Adolf Hitler? Or, at a more everyday level, why are so many people homeless in the middle of affluent western cities? The traditional western (Christian) answer has been that they are the victims of oppression, greed, exploitation and injustice. People like this have been wounded because of other people's uncaring attitudes. They are not sinners, responsible for their own misery. They are sinned against, and as losers are the victims of somebody else's apparent success. But the typical New Age answer to such questions is rather different. The traditional terminology of sin has been scrapped, but we are still being told that people have only themselves to blame for their own fate. Jack Underhill's comment in *Life Times Magazine* sums it up neatly: 'There are no victims in this life or any other. No mistakes. No wrong paths. No winners. No losers. Accept that, and then take responsibility for making your life what you want it to be'.[8]

In other words, whoever and whatever you are, it is because you have chosen to be that way. This is another theme that dominates many of today's top training techniques. Probably the dominant theme. For not too many corporate managers are interested in ideology and historical perspectives. But they are desperate for efficiency, both for themselves and for their companies. At a time of increasing stress and pressure, faced with unprecedented personal challenges, everybody wants to know that they can cope with it all. Not just cope, but shine through it – to become super-efficient, super-happy, and super-confident. If possible, to become like Superman himself – imbued with that poise and confidence that only extraterrestrials ever seem to have, sharing in the cosmic wisdom of the ages that will help put all our problems in their true perspective. If we are honest, we will admit that we all have this dream. And New Age therapies can make it come true. In the words of Marilyn Ferguson, 'You can break through old limits, past inertia and fear, to levels of fulfilment that once seemed impossible . . . to richness of choice, freedom, human closeness. You can be more productive, confident, comfortable with insecurity. Problems can be experienced as challenges, a chance for renewal, rather than stress. Habitual defensiveness and worry can fall away . . .'[9]

In this world of practical problem-solving, commonplace cliches and homespun philosophies combine with hard-headed business acumen and half-truths about modern science and so-called brain technologies to make up courses on 'personal management'. Courses that, it is claimed, will radically transform the typical executive from someone who is half-hearted and defeatist to a super-person reborn in a new, dynamic image that will revolutionize both the individual and the corporation.

A bewildering array of techniques for self-improvement are regularly on offer, ranging from the merely bizarre to the potentially dangerous. 'We've all experienced the tiredness and frustration caused by traffic jams and long distance driving . . .' Well, we have, haven't we? Which is why the advertiser assures us we need a thing called 'Drive Alert' – an electronic gadget based on 'aroma science', that plugs into your car's cigarette lighter to improve concentration, increase alertness and relieve stress. If you read the small print, you'll find it will even 'make you a better and safer driver'. Which it won't, of course. If you can't drive to start with, then ten pounds' worth of electrical hocus-pocus is unlikely to make much difference.

If you're not too keen on the idea of driving along the highway in an altered state of consciousness, you might like to try the Crystal Ray – a small device about the size of a cigarette lighter that contains a crystal and delivers what is alleged to be a healing electrical shock. You can even get a book to help you find personal fulfilment and satisfaction. You don't read much? Well, don't worry – that's not going to be necessary to enjoy the full effects of this particular volume. *The Ultimate Super Will Power*, by Japanese writer Katao Ishii, can do it all for you. Quite literally. 'This book is permeated with will power' the author claims. 'Please try holding this book against any part of your body that may be causing you pain or discomfort. That pain or discomfort should go away. Also, if you simply put this book in your bag or brief case, the eighth dimensional power generated by the book will bring you happiness and good fortune.' If it doesn't work, there is a money-back guarantee!

CHANGING THE WAY WE THINK

The executive toys of the nineties? Of course. But other trendy techniques raise more serious questions. The eighties were arguably the decade of mass involvement in sports and physical recreation. Almost everybody became a fitness freak. Especially people who were kids in the sixties, but were approaching their forties and wanted to prove to themselves and everyone else that they were not physically past it. Now, in a new decade, they're not so sure, which probably goes some way to explain why suddenly it's the brain's turn for some development. Just as physical exercise has been taken over by mechanical contraptions of every conceivable size and shape (how did people exercise before the invention of the multi-gym and the exercise bike, I wonder?), you can also buy time – and, allegedly, self-discovery – at the brain gymnasium.

If you've never done it before, then a few sessions with a thing called the Mind Mirror is probably as good a place as any to make a start. It's also one of the cheapest therapies, at about £40–50 for five sessions. What can it do for you? 'Think of it as a kind of sophisticated bathroom scale,' one devotee told me. 'You probably already know that you've put on a few pounds, or lost a few pounds, but the scales just confirm it. The Mind Mirror does the same for your brain. You have a good idea whether you're stressed or relaxed, but the Mind Mirror defines it for you, helps you to explore your own mental state so you can decide what to do about it.' Technically, the Mind Mirror is an electro-encephalo-graph, or EEG machine. A complex piece of electronic circuitry that can detect electrical rhythms passing through the brain and analyze them into different frequencies.

This is all based on established scientific knowledge. Medics have known for a long time that the readings produced on an EEG have some correlation with brain states. When people get wired up to one of these machines, the screen in front of them simply reports on what is going on inside their brains. The constantly changing electrochemical reactions in the brain – signals commonly called 'brainwaves' – are picked up through electrodes attached to the scalp and other parts of the body. These brainwaves occur in different frequencies, known as alpha, beta, theta and delta, each of which roughly corresponds to a particular state of mind. When we are wide awake and very active, beta is generally the dominant brainwave pattern. In a relaxed state with eyes closed, we can expect more alpha frequencies to be present. The more we relax, the slower our brainwaves become. When we're drowsy, they are mostly alpha, but with a little theta creeping in – and if we're in a very deep sleep, then delta brainwaves will be the predominant pattern.

When you get hooked up to one of these devices, it acts as a kind of psychic looking-glass, to let you see the electrical forces at work in your brain. It doesn't actually do anything for you, except help to confirm the way you're probably feeling anyhow. Hence the name 'biofeedback', because it simply feeds you with information from your own life systems. Once you have the information, then it's up to you to do something about it. The machine tells you that you're over-anxious, and you need to relax. It trains you to recognize small changes in your psycho-physiology, helps you to be more aware of your body, and thereby tells you it's time to engage in whatever therapy may help that particular state. Followers of the biofeedback technique claim it can help them to evolve into higher states of consciousness and develop creativity, and to control stress-related conditions such as migraine, insomnia and hypertension.

Scientific opinion is divided on the usefulness of all this. The technology can definitely describe electrical impulses in the brain. But whether this is directly related to mind states is an open question. There is also the fact that the circuitry needs to be extremely sophisticated –

and therefore costly – to give a dependable result. A hospital brain scanner capable of distinguishing electrical currents between the left and right sides of the brain typically costs in excess of a million pounds sterling, and that kind of money is simply not available even to the brain technicians of the New Age.

Even supposing it works, the Mind Mirror doesn't actually do anything for you. It's only a diagnostic tool: you have to discover and apply the remedies for yourself. Most of the time, people find there is little they can do to bring about a conscious change in their brainwave patterns. So there has to be a big demand for any device that will claim to do it all for you. Flashing lights and intense sound, combined with sensory deprivation, have always been the basic ingredients of brainwashing techniques in prison camps around the world. They also play a big part in many of the latest mind management courses. Ever heard of binaural beats? Sound engineers sometimes call it 'phasing', and spend most of their time desperately trying to avoid it. It is a simple phenomenon. If you play two notes simultaneously at very slightly different frequencies, you produce a warbling sound. According to some contemporary brain mechanics, these peculiar noises hold the key to personal self-discovery, fulfilment and transformation.

The theory is that sound affects the signals passing through your brain. You wear a set of headphones and the frequency of the noise you hear in one earpiece is slightly different to the frequency of the noise in the other. The warbling effect of the binaural beat will resonate through the brain and, it is claimed, drive it into other dimensions of psychic activity. Different types of beat allegedly correspond with the various electrical brainwave patterns, and by listening to them you can change your own brainwaves. For hyperactive or stressed people with a high concentration of beta rhythms, an electrical machine that could induce particular states of relaxation by changing beta to theta or delta would have obvious benefits. There are a whole range of commercially produced tapes available for this very purpose, all of which can be played on a normal stereo system. According to their promoters, they can do a lot of different things for you: they can help you to lose weight, stop smoking, improve your concentration, rejuvenate your immune system, supercharge your sexual performance, increase your self-confidence, boost your creativity – or just make you incredibly rich and happy. Whatever your need, there is a tape to meet it. What's more, you can share the benefits with others as well. Imagine you're a teacher in school, and your children regularly come in from the playground in an excitable state – all you have to do is use a theta-delta-type binaural beat for a few minutes, perhaps in combination with an audio recording of surf or music, and you can calm them down almost instantaneously. You can also, it is claimed, speed up their learning processes in a similar way.

Of course, not everybody sees it like this. If you can turn an innocent-looking stereo player into an effective tool for military-style brainwashing, that could be dangerous in the wrong hands. Brainwashing may be an emotive and alarmist term to use, but so far as the actual techniques are concerned, these devices use very similar methods. Sensory deprivation, in which all influences from the outside world are excluded, invariably features somewhere, often in an apparently benign way, using a VCR machine and an ordinary TV set. It's even possible to buy a portable mind machine styled to look like a Walkman, but with a pair of special spectacles attached.

This device will transmit mind-changing signals to your eyes and ears as you walk along the street, or work in the office, thus ensuring permanently altered states of consciousness – or so the inventors claim. A similar experience is on sale at the many flotation centres now springing up all around the western world. Here, lying in darkness, flat on your back in a tank of dense salt water, with your ears sealed with wax plugs, and being gently bombarded with sounds of the natural world or with New Age music, it is possible to enter altered states of consciousness which, it is claimed, will reduce stress, enhance creativity, improve intelligence and in general make you a better person. Floaters claim that this induces the brain to secrete substances called endorphines into the bloodstream. These are natural hormone-like drugs produced by the brain, and they act as a mild form of tranquillizer. This is why it is worth paying for the experience – typically, in Britain, about £25 for an hour. Of course, in the labour camps of totalitarian regimes you could have the same experiences for nothing!

Some practitioners claim all this has a very ancient origin. They say it is at least as old as the Roman Empire, whose dictators regularly sent their servants out to bring in a continuous supply of electric fish – eels, rayfish, catfish and the like. These were then applied to their heads to induce altered states of consciousness. But today these mind-altering techniques are marketed as up-beat, hi-tech, modern discoveries – a means of breaking down the barriers between the left and right hemispheres of the brain. A typical advert claims that 'both sides of your brain become synchronized and receptive to suggestions . . . you are then receptive to new programming to change your beliefs and circumstances'.

But can it be so easy? Psychiatrists are not so sure. We

know that brainwaves exist, of course, and there is some kind of connexion between them and our moods. When eastern mystics put themselves into different states of consciousness, those states – or, rather, their electro-chemical effects – can be tracked. But there is no evidence that it works the opposite way round, that by feeding in particular electrical impulses you can actually change anything in the mind. One psychiatrist put it to me quite simply: 'These devices are not doing what they claim to the brain. The situation's a lot more complicated than that kind of over-simplified picture. It's impossible to say that there's a one-to-one relationship between brainwaves and mental states. People can be relaxed without showing much alpha activity – and conversely, there's no way that putting a person's brainwaves into an alpha will necessarily make them more relaxed'. Yet in spite of such professional scepticism about the basis of mind manipulation, there's no doubt that something happens when people are wired up to these machines. Used on the wrong people, some of them can readily induce unconsciousness, epileptic fits, or worse.

So what is going on? In so far as anything happens, most psychiatrists are of the opinion that it is psycho-logical, not physiological. Sensory deprivation of one kind or another is involved in all these techniques, whether it is literally the exclusion of all external sights, sounds and smells, or something as simple as lying on a couch wearing a pair of earphones. It is a well-documented fact that once you isolate yourself from the outside world, you get changes in perception. You get funny feelings, you hear different voices, you may even see strange visions. The brain certainly functions differently, and is also highly suggestible in such a state. If you have a belief system of some sort, then it's quite likely this will become overwhelming and you may start to see and hear things that your beliefs suggest you will. If you have a skilled operator, making suggestions about how to cope with stress or whatever, then this too might lead to some kind of new experience of yourself. But in this case, it is more likely to be the person running the technique, acting as a sort of counsellor (perhaps without realizing it), who sorts out the problems, rather than the fancy electrical hardware. There is also the matter of group dynamics. Many of these techniques – especially when used as part of a training course – involve groups of people together, and mutual support and counselling almost certainly play a significant part in their results.

MIND OVER MATTER

If you're still with me, you might reasonably wonder if we haven't been wandering through some rather off-beat territory. Certainly, not all these therapies are used in every self-improvement course. But in the end, they are all based on a widely held belief: that mind is more real than matter, and that you can somehow control things or events on the basis of that. In practical everyday terms, that means you can be or do anything you want. Nothing is barred to you, if you want it hard enough. If you're a failure, then that's because you think negatively, you have low expectations of yourself. This concept was popularized earlier this century by the American writer Norman Vincent Peale's book, *The Power of Positive Thinking*, and historically it has close links to many of the nineteenth-century antecedents of the New Age Movement.

Like so much of what we have looked at here, it has just enough truth in it to demand that we take it seriously.

There can be no denying that there are many depressed and defeated people around in modern society. They are not just defeated, but defeatist. People with a very poor self-image, who have convinced themselves that they are so unworthy and useless that any enterprise they get involved in is doomed to failure before they even get started. They always expect failure – whether in the world of business, or in their personal, social and family life. The reasons for such negative feelings are extremely diverse. Sometimes life seems to have dealt them such a bad hand of cards that they actually begin with inbuilt weaknesses in physical or social skills. More often, they have been victimized and bullied by other people who have sought to use them for their own selfish ends. Occasionally, their misery is compounded by their own strongly held religious beliefs – beliefs that encourage them to believe they are terrible sinners, with whom God is angry, and for whom there can be neither forgiveness nor recovery. Whenever they think of themselves, words like 'original sin' and 'total depravity' immediately spring to mind, and they find it impossible to see themselves in any sort of good light. Prominent elements in all this emotional baggage are likely to be poor childhood memories, inadequate bonding with parents, guilt about the past, and sexual hang-ups of one sort or another – all of which lead inexorably and repeatedly to personal breakdown and failure. New Ager Marilyn Ferguson is perfectly right when she writes, 'High intention cannot coexist with a low self-image. Only those who are awake, connected, and motivated can add to the synergy of an organization'.[10]

Because of our historic western experience of the Christian tradition, Christianity is again often criticized as a major cause of problems like this. It cannot be denied that low self-esteem often goes hand-in-hand with certain forms of Christianity, notably the Calvinist outlook and certain aspects of sectarian Evangelicalism. There is no question that many people find themselves put down because of the religious outlook either of other people or themselves – and we shall need to return to this issue in our final chapter. Here, let's restrict ourselves to the practical question of how we can break out of this negative mind-set. A typical New Age answer is that we all choose to be who we are and that the different choices we make in our different lives reflect our spiritual needs at that particular point in our continuing existence. It may be suggested that we are unable to make helpful choices as a result of some blockage or imbalance in the flow of life-energy through our physical body, and we need therapy to enable us to tune in to our inner spirit. These therapies might typically range from simple visualization techniques to enable us to come to terms with past failures, through regular psychiatric treatments to alleviate guilt, to more overtly mystical and spiritual procedures that may involve spirit entities of various kinds.

We have already looked closely at some of these subjects, and noted serious deficiences in the entire worldview that they represent. But what is wrong with thinking big as a means to making yourself more successful than you are now? I remember discussing the Olympic Games with a manager who had just returned from a course based on this approach to positive thinking. He was like many business people: middle class, middle aged, slightly balding – and certainly overweight. As we talked in his office he laid back in his plush armchair and said (slightly self-consciously, but certainly seriously): 'You know, I now realize that I could be out there on that

running track – up front, along with the world's best.
Sure, there are some powerful energies around. But if I
was in a race against Carl Lewis and lost, it would only be
because I didn't want to win enough.' But of course, just
thinking big and positive isn't enough. It's actually quite
easy to delude yourself. Managers all around the world
are being trained to begin each day with 'affirmations',
telling themselves things like, 'I am a super salesperson,
and grow every day in every way . . . If it's going to be, it's
up to me,' or 'imagination times vividness equals reality
on the sub-conscious level.' But reality is not that simple.
If as a matter of fact you're a rotten manager, then no
amount of positive affirmation is going to change that.
Or, as one psychologist put it to me: 'I think all of us are
aware that we never actually use all our talents, that there
are a lot more things we could do and be. But the notion
that by changing the way our brain operates, or by
relaxing completely, or being stimulated in some particular way, somehow we're going to discover reserves of
creativity we didn't know we had – that's just nonsense.
The trouble is you can only be creative if you've got the
stuff inside you to start with.' Somehow, I don't think my
friend who believed he could beat Carl Lewis actually
had the necessary physical equipment to do it! If we are
ever to be balanced individuals, then psychological good
health has to start with facing the facts about ourselves –
not ignoring them or pretending they are different than
they are.

There is also the problem of exploitation associated
with many of these techniques. Christians are not the
only ones to be concerned about this. The *Wall Street
Journal* for 9 January 1989 reported a lawsuit brought
against the Atlanta firm, DeKalb Farmers Market Inc.,
by eight of its former employees – all of them fired or

persuaded to resign after objecting to a course called The Forum. This is a development of a programme originally called 'est' (Erhard Seminars Training), after its originator Werner Erhard. It has been widely promoted in business training, and thousands of people have used it to achieve altered states of consciousness. It consists of a series of intensive sessions of something like sixteen hours each, with only limited movement allowed, minimal food and toilet breaks, and no smoking, writing or talking. The instructor humiliates the group by telling them their lives are in a mess. They don't know how to cope, and have lost sight of their real life objectives. As the participants sit there for hour after hour, they are gradually worn down, both physically and emotionally, until they are ready for the enlightening message that they alone are responsible for everything. They are, in effect, gods who have created the circumstances they now live in, and have within them the power to change things. Not surprisingly, in the surrealistic atmosphere created by such psychological bombardment, many of the DeKalb workers felt they were being manipulated and subjected to a form of brainwashing. All the elements of constriction and sensory deprivation used by classical spymasters certainly seemed to be present. Dong Shik Kim, a Korean who was a supervisor at the Market, spoke of 'emotional confessions, psychological conditioning and programming. . . equivalent to being "born again"', while Ranjana Sampat, a book-keeper and a Hindu, claimed that she was asked to 'confess' intimate details of her life, including sexual relations. Nor is this an isolated example. The last decade has seen hundreds of similar cases going through the courts, and many more allegations being settled outside the legal process.

Perhaps the most serious aspect to all this is a question

Getting it All Together

we have already come across. Quite simply, if we have all chosen to be who and what we are, then no one needs to have a social conscience. Is it a good thing for each of us to have the freedom to live life purely by choosing who we want to be? Marilyn Ferguson quotes with approval an engineer who commented, 'Do things in the spirit of design research. Be willing to accept a mistake and redesign. There is no failure.'[11] It is not hard to see why that would appeal to the New Age mind-set, for the view that ultimately there is neither good nor evil fits in well with the holistic view of eastern mysticism. But it raises enormous questions of practical morality when we try and apply it to real-life situations.

Life is not actually that simple. We interact with other people, and our mistakes can often have the most far-reaching impact on their lives. The idea that we should all stand on our own two feet and take responsibility for ourselves may sound like the ultimate in personal freedom. It is easy to say that everyone should be free to make their own choices, and that we should all allow others to choose their own options, without necessarily embracing them ourselves. Sometimes, it works. Of course, there are occasionally dilemmas involved – on abortion, for example – though we can often manage to accommodate even them without diminishing the personal right to choose. But freedom to choose is not always quite as straightforward as it sounds. What if somebody wants to choose to be a Hitler? Should they have freedom to do that? And if not, why not? Did he just make a mistake, that he would have tried to correct given another chance? Or is it the case that there was nothing wrong with his choices anyway, and his decision to be a dictator and mass murderer was the right one for him? Choosing to be who I want to be can have disastrous knock-on effects for others in the wider community. To suppose that the disadvantaged and marginalized people of today's world have chosen to be that way is arrogant and selfish. How can we take seriously an outlook claiming to be committed to a holistic world vision, when it takes such a selfish stand on social ethics?

And how can the management consultants who run these unorthodox training courses claim that this is nothing to do with New Age thinking, when it is all so clearly similar to the kind of messages allegedly being received from discarnate entities through trance channeling, and when crystals are regularly handed out to participants in such training courses? In their book, *Channeling: The Intuitive Connection*, William H. Kautz and Melanie Branon make a direct connexion, and as they look into the future they expect to see the channeling of spirit guides incorporated into business education 'side by side with conventional, rational instruction'.[12] From what I have seen, we are already halfway there. The New Age worldview is more widespread than many realize, and it can only be a matter of time before management trainers are introducing executives to their own spirit guides. After all, the 'Experience Astrology' brochure promises exactly what modern businesses are looking for: 'Experience clarity, discover purpose, recognize challenges and opportunities, and take effective action'.

Is it any wonder that multinational corporations are often insensitive to the needs of people, when this sort of belief about mind power forms the core of some of the most popular training programmes, in which managers are constantly being told that 'You are who you choose to be.' If that's really true, then it's going to be bad news for many of the rest of us. The individualistic and self-centred stand-on-your-own-two-feet mentality, far from being a formula for harmony and efficiency, sounds suspiciously like one of the more negative legacies of that Enlightenment thinking that has helped to create the discord and fragmentation that is so clearly in evidence all around us. If the New Age is going to be more of the same, then we can do without it.

Chapter 7

WHAT IS THE NEW AGE SAYING TO THE CHURCH?

*I*N the last two or three years I must have led hundreds of workshops on the New Age Movement, and one question never fails to come up. 'Isn't it all just a passing fad?' someone will ask hopefully, perhaps adding that since the whole thing seems so unbelievable they think I've made most of it up, or at the very least taken a good deal of liberty with the truth. But such people are living with their heads in the sand. Take a quick look at any bookstore or magazine outlet, and you will see that the fastest-growing section is the one headed 'New Age'. Turn on the television, and as likely as not there will be a chat show featuring a leading New Ager, either as guest or presenter. Go to check out the latest fashion accessories, and the New Age will be lurking there too. Or visit the supermarket where you will very probably be encouraged to dip into your wallet by the soothing cadences of New Age music. Christians who imagine this will all fade away overnight are indulging in their own forms of fantasy games. The fact that the Church does not know how to react to the New Age will not lead to its diminution. Quite the reverse. As we progress through the nineties, through to the dawn not just of a new century but also of a new millenium in human history, with all the heightened expectation that will create, we can only expect the spiritual clamour to become even louder. Unless Christians realize what is happening, and enter into a constructive engagement with the questions now being raised within the New Age Movement, we will only reinforce the dominant, negative image that most westerners already have of the Church. They see it as a spiritual dinosaur in a state of terminal decline, as a part of the past, and for that very reason accountable for the mess our world is in, and not deserving to share in setting the spiritual agenda for the future.

Like it or not, the New Age is here to stay. Not least because its leading advocates are mostly influential people in positions of leadership and authority in business, government and education. As a result, its influence is all-pervasive. The New Age Movement has a profound effect on the food we eat, the books we read and the music we hear; it influences the way in which we heal the sick, comfort the emotionally ill, teach our children, manage our companies and think about the environment. Of course, only a relatively small number of people overall would self-consciously apply the label 'New Age' to themselves – and some of the Movement's more esoteric manifestations are undoubtedly minority inter-ests by any standards. If you were to take everything that has been described in this book – not to mention the myriads of techniques and mythologies that have not featured at all – and ask, 'Who believes all this?' the answer would probably be 'No one.' But if you take more general soundings about the various elements that go to make up the New Age mishmash and ask, 'Who believes *some* of this?' the outcome will be radically different. For one way or another, the general outlook which we identify as the New Age is now probably the predominant worldview among western people. The folks next door, or those you work with, are definitely likely to have far more in common with New Age thinking than with anything remotely resembling mainstream Christianity. That does not necessarily make them New Agers in the technical sense, for not everyone accepts the total New Age worldview. But many people drift in and out of it, picking up elements that are useful to them at particular points in life – which means they are at least interested in what is going on.

CHANGING BELIEFS AND CHRISTIAN ATTITUDES

In April 1990, the *San Francisco Chronicle* commissioned a major poll of religious beliefs among the residents of northern California.[1] It came up with some staggering facts. It was entirely predictable that 87% would say they believed in 'God' in some kind of spiritual form. Most Americans do. But it was a surprise to learn that only 44% defined 'God' as 'the personal God written about in the Bible, who watches over us and answers our prayers'. The same number preferred to believe in 'a spiritual force that is alive in the universe and connects all living things', while even more (57%) agreed that 'nature or Mother Earth has its own kind of wisdom, a planetary consciousness of its own'. A further 38% believed it was possible to make contact with discarnate spirits, with 24% believing in reincarnation. While a massive 62% maintained that it was possible to realize full human potential by entering into altered states of consciousness – something that 46% had actually tried for themselves on either a casual or regular basis. Since northern

Californians are just as religious as other Americans, with 72% of them belonging to some branch of the Christian Church, you can draw your own conclusions: New Age is here to stay, and is well established among the Christian population.

There has not been a comparable recent poll in Britain, and if there was the figures would almost certainly not be quite the same. But that is not good news for the churches, for Christianity itself has a much weaker base of support in the UK than in the USA, with considerably fewer people having any regular contact at all with the Church. The only thing we can be certain about is that movements that begin in California never stay there for long. It used to be said that it took ten years for Californian values to spread to the eastern states, and then another ten for them to cross the Atlantic. But that was before the day of instant communications and rapid exchange of information. For a generation whose values have been formed by *Star Wars*, *Superman*, *ET*, and *He-Man*, the New Age philosophy is the most obvious way to understand things.

The New Age has already penetrated the minds and hearts of the young adults of Europe in a big way. Statistics gathered in 1989, before the reunion of Germany, showed that in the former West Germany alone, there were some 90,000 registered witches, compared with only 30,000 Christian clergy of all denominations. Of the 2,000 religious books published every year in Britain, something like one in four will be on a New Age topic. Acid House parties are regularly attended by thousands of young people who are looking for altered states of consciousness. Admittedly, they are likely to be using designer drugs such as 'Ecstasy', rather than the sophisticated psycho-spiritual technologies that are more popular among people of their parents' generation. But though New Age leader Marilyn Ferguson warns against drug abuse, she nevertheless lists psychedelic drugs as one of four groups of 'intentional triggers of transformative experiences'.[2] Similar cultural shifts are happening all over the western world. The only surprising thing is that the Church has apparently been caught unawares. As long ago as 1930, Ronald Knox made this prediction in a sermon preached to students at Oxford University: *EXAMPLE*

> there is a new kind of paganism springing up. . . The danger now is not polytheism, but pantheism. Men will agree with us that God exists, will agree with us that he is one; but when we examine their meaning more closely we find that they do not think of him as almighty . . . Rather, they will tell you that as the body of man and the soul of man form one single being, so God and the universe form one single being. God is the soul and the universe the body: it is no more possible to think of God as existing without the universe than to think of the universe as existing without God.

Rephrase that using inclusive language, call it the New Age, and you have a pretty accurate description of what is going on today. Yet Christians have very divided attitudes towards it all. On the one hand, some believe there is no such thing as the New Age Movement – and so naturally they need do nothing about it – while others see it as a monstrous threat, and are arming themselves for a spiritual confrontation of massive proportions. They have convinced themselves that if at the last great battle of Armageddon Christianity will not actually be fighting the New Age, then it will be fighting something related to it. They see the emergence of the New Age as itself a sign that Armageddon is at hand, with the New Age and its leaders as demonic and satanic – perhaps even being the Antichrist. Standing before some 1,500 leaders of conservative American Christianity at the 1990 convention of National Religious Broadcasters, TV evangelist Pat Robertson lowered his voice to a throaty whisper as he looked into the future and issued a dark prophecy: 'There is something coming from the East,' he warned. 'It's a modified version of Hinduism. It's called the New Age. It's sweeping into American businesses, the classrooms of America, infiltrating into Europe. It's even in the Soviet Union.' He went on to denounce it as 'blatant demonism', and called for a Christian crusade against it. He is not alone in his opinions. Even in the San Francisco poll, 26% of the general population said they believed that 'Satan or some demonic power is at work behind a lot of the New Age Movement', while a further 14% sat on the fence saying they didn't know whether or not that was true – but implying that they could easily be persuaded it was.

Other Christian writers are so strident in their attacks on the New Age that they make Pat Robertson look like a woolly, middle-of-the-road liberal – no mean feat in itself. They denounce the New Age Movement as some kind of take-over bid for world government, even claiming that it is related to an underground resurgence of the Nazi movement. Christian bookstores are all but swamped with the torrent of literature heaping vitriolic condemnation on everything and everyone that can vaguely be labelled as 'New Age'. Such publications – though claiming to be Christian – seem to have a good deal more to say about demons than about God, and regularly denounce almost everything in today's world as satanic and demonic. Channeling of spirit guides, environmental concern, alternative medicine, even the Christian charismatic movement – they are all being condemned as a deliberate attempt by evil supernatural forces to undermine society. The best-selling novels of Frank Peretti have sent Christians all over the western world scurrying through the corridors of power in government and city hall, looking for the tell-tale signs of New Age manipulation.

Protestant Fundamentalists are not the only ones engaged in this particular war of words. There is a growing unease in the Roman Catholic Church about the influence of New Age ideas. In a twenty-five page document dated 14 December 1989 and approved by the Pope, Cardinal Joseph Ratzinger, head of the Vatican Congregation for the Doctrine of the Faith, warned bishops around the world to be on the lookout for the infiltration of New Age thinking into their churches. He claimed that, among other things, New Age practices can lead to 'moral deviations' and 'psychic disturbances' and can 'degenerate into a cult of the body and can lead surreptitiously to considering all bodily sensation as spiritual experience'. But it will take more than warnings from the Vatican before the Catholic faithful know how to respond. Zen, yoga, dream work and other themes drawn from the New Age mixture regularly feature in the programmes of retreat centres. At the Holy Names College, a Roman Catholic campus in Oakland, California, students of the Institute in Culture and Creation Spirituality follow courses that include Native American shamanism, witchcraft, eco-feminism and mysticism, as well as more traditional Christian concerns. Matthew Fox, the dynamic and radical priest who founded the Centre, has been condemned by Ratzinger as 'dangerous and deviant', and was officially banned from public speaking for a year by his own Dominican Order. Ironically, while the Vatican has been trying to have Fox silenced, others have been alleging that the Pope himself has New Age sympathies, because back in 1986 he met with people of other faiths at Assisi!

Virtually identical conflicts have surfaced in Britain over various developments in the Church of England, and stinging accusations have been directed against the Anglican Communion's top leaders. Former Archbishop of Canterbury, Dr Robert Runcie, was condemned as a covert New Ager because of his involvement in services relating to environmental and inter-faith concerns. Many Anglican cathedrals have come under attack for hosting 'Festivals of Creation' to draw attention to the environmental crisis. The World Council of Churches has also been vilified for its programme on Justice, Peace and the Integrity of Creation. Even the Queen has not escaped criticism. In 1990, over 76,000 signatures were gathered for a petition complaining about her involvement in a Westminster Abbey celebration of Commonwealth Day alongside the leaders of other countries and other (non-Christian) religious faiths.

Saint James' Church in London's Piccadilly has been identified as a major breeding ground for New Age views. The particular cause of concern is a programme of 'alternative ministry' that the church's rector, the Rev Donald Reeves, has been running for some time. Alongside traditional Anglican worship, he hosts seminars and workshops on such topics as alternative healing, meditation and earth mysteries. There are also celebrations of the cycles of the moon and concerts of New Age music. None of this activity is clandestine or surreptitious. The church's own advertising material says quite openly that 'Alternative Ministry at St James'

Church in Piccadilly is concerned with what is known as New Age thinking', and goes on to say that 'these are ideas which provide creative and spiritual alternatives to currently accepted western thought'. The leaders of many of these events are brought in from outside the church, and some have close connexions with mainstream New Age groups such as the Theosophical Society or the Findhorn Community. There has been no shortage of people ready to accuse the rector of the church of heresy. To which he responds that, far from undermining Christian faith, what he is promoting is actually a form of evangelism. Writing in the British magazine *Prophecy Today* in May 1989, he began by denying that his church actually endorses everything in the New Age, and then claimed, 'I know of many who have found Christ through the hospitality we have offered' – though with the qualification that this is 'a difficult ministry, easily misunderstood and sometimes, as I have often said and freely admit, we have made mistakes . . .' Archbishop Robert Runcie seems to have a good deal of sympathy with this view. In a 1989 speech to a conference of senior Evangelical Anglican clergy, he claimed that in responding to the New Age 'a spirit of engagement rather than of condemnation will serve us best' – though he also hedged his bets by adding that 'engagement might sometimes take the form of conflict or struggle'. American Episcopalian George Gallup Jr – highly experienced in interpreting cultural and social trends – reinforces that position, with his warning that the New Age is

a serious threat to Christianity. It appeals to those who have little religious grounding but are looking for meaning in their lives. Its methods – such as meditation – are fine. But its ends are the glorification of self, not God. Christianity and New Age cannot possibly exist side-by-side.

The fact is that those western Christians who have taken the New Age Movement seriously are divided in their attitude towards it. But most members of the Church know little about it, though they have probably come across it under one guise or another. Many of them are likely to be part of it, without realizing what is going on, as they follow the free-market philosophy of our day, and choose their spiritual diet from a variety of sources. It surprises me how many people worship at a mainline church on a Sunday, and then practise yoga meditation for self-awareness during the week, while consulting extraterrestrial spirit entities for personal guidance on all their major life decisions.

It is not my intention here to take sides in this debate. It has become polarized in an unhelpful way, and in any case much of it (at least on the Protestant side) seems to be fuelled by the internal politics of Evangelical Christianity. It is certainly striking that when Evangelical preachers claim (as increasing numbers do) that following their particular spiritual therapies will make you healthy, wealthy and wise, no one ever seems to denounce *them* as New Agers, despite the fact that their crusades and TV programmes regularly look more like motivational seminars than mainstream Christian worship – constantly extolling the virtues of the power of the mind and will over material reality, and suggesting that with enough faith you can change anything. Nor can we ignore the fact that the techniques and methodologies of some strands in the charismatic movement look suspiciously similar to occult practices. Indeed, in a striking address delivered to the 1989 meeting of the American Academy of Religion, Phillip Lucas of the University of California at Santa Barbara suggested that the charismatic movement and the New Age are just different manifestations of what is in reality the same spiritual movement. I must confess that I have personally met a disturbingly large number of people who started in the charismatic movement, and then when they became disillusioned with that, moved into hard-core New Age spirituality.

CHALLENGING THE CHURCH

Debates like this will likely continue for a long time. But it is all too easy for them to become a comfortable, in-house diversion, directing the attention of Christians away from the actual challenge that New Age thinking presents to today's Church. In the long run that would be counter-productive, and ultimately unhelpful to the Christian faith. Of course, many aspects of the New Age Movement give cause for legitimate concern, and we should not adopt a naive and uncritical attitude towards it. But neither should we dismiss it by jumping to the complacent conclusion that all New Agers are demon-possessed. Such a judgement would be inaccurate and untrue. It would also be dangerous – dangerous for the Church, that is.

Dangerous because it lulls Christians into a false sense of security. If the New Age is all just the work of the devil, then by definition there is very little any of us can do about it: we'll just have to leave God to sort it all out in some other cosmic sphere. We might hold up our hands in horror, but we can have no sort of engagement with what is going on.

Such a judgement would also be dangerous because it

is likely to set up an uncompromising and unnecessary opposition between the followers of Christ and other genuine spiritual searchers of our generation. The words of James Sire say it all so eloquently:

> A siege mentality is at work. Those who hold cultic ideas are seen as the enemy, the great threat to humanity, to Christians, even some seem to suggest, to God himself . . . So in response anything goes: innuendo, name-calling, backhanded remarks, assumption of the worst motives on the part of the cult believers. And thus the Christian dehumanizes the enemy and shoots him like a dog. But the Christian in this process is himself dehumanized . . .[3]

The overwhelming majority of people who get involved in New Age spirituality are engaged in a serious search for God. If anything, they are likely to be more open to a radical life-changing encounter with Christ than are many Christians. But they will not be won over to Christ by confrontation. They will be reached most effectively as Christians learn to follow the example of Jesus himself, who consistently challenged people by standing alongside them. This is something the church has forgotten. We don't know how to stand alongside people without compromising our own faith. And we don't know how to challenge people effectively either. If we did, the Church in the West would not be what it is today.

Christians need to face the fact that the New Age Movement is presenting some hard questions that demand an answer. It would be foolish to deny that the New Age analysis of our present crisis and of the reasons why we have got where we are has much to be said for it. Sure, it is programmatic and, to a degree, exaggerated. It ignores many factors in western culture over the last two or three centuries, and makes generalizations about subjects – such as science – that are in reality very complex. But the broad argument – that we have lost our way because we have gone spiritually off-course by viewing things in a mechanistic and reductionist frame of reference – is right on target. Those who are unafraid of facing the truth about themselves can do little but accept this – whether they are Christians or New Agers. That is how it is in modern western culture.

Moreover, the New Age agenda runs strikingly parallel to the Christian agenda at many points. Concern for personal freedom and maturity, for the environment, for peace and justice, for self-discovery, for a holistic view of life – these are all things that Christians should be committed to in any case, because they are an integral part of the message of Jesus himself. The major difference between the Christian faith and New Age spirituality is not to be found in our social, economic, political or environmental hopes and aspirations, but in our beliefs about how these goals can be achieved. Whereas the New Age outlook identifies the basic problem as an alienated or undeveloped consciousness, Christians take evil and suffering seriously, and affirm that the basic problem is a moral one, not a metaphysical one. Sin, if you like. But Christians have a further challenge to face. Many of them think that sin is something other people do. But New Agers frequently accuse the Church of being a part of the problem, and not the solution to it. We need to treat this criticism with the seriousness it deserves, assess it in the light of our own knowledge of God through Jesus Christ, and then do something about it. It will be a provocative – even painful – business to do so. It will demand repentance, a loss of face and a willingness to change, because it is true that we have often failed even to try to live according to the spirit of Christ. Spiritual integrity demands that we admit as much, and renew our own faith commitment in that light.

To admit all this in no way implies endorsement of all that is going on in the New Age Movement. But we have to be big enough to agree with New Agers when they are right. And when their actions and attitudes lead – as they often do – to values that are central to the Gospel, then we should stand alongside them. Remember the words of Jesus himself: 'You will know them by their fruits' (Matthew 7:16). By that criterion, many New Agers are a lot closer to God's Kingdom than some of their Christian critics are. Having said that, there are some things on which the New Age worldview is simply wrong. It is wrong when it affirms that we are all God, or all equal with God – and some New Agers have themselves rejected this view. It is wrong when it suggests that 'going within' will solve all our problems. Looking within has been the cause of most of them. It is wrong when it refuses to recognize the reality of undeserved suffering, and the presence of evil in our world. And it is wrong when it denies that there can ever be absolute values and beliefs, emphasizing instead what seems 'right for you'.

How then can Christians begin to deal with some of the issues that are raised by all this? This takes us to the heart of today's spiritual search, and identifies very precisely the Church's predicament.

FACTS AND FAITH

G. K. Chesterton once remarked that 'When a man ceases to believe in God, he doesn't believe in nothing, he believes in anything.' This is a most appropriate comment on much that is going on under the guise of the

New Age Movement. People are rightly questioning the
rationalistic attitude that has brought the western world
to its present crisis. But in the process they are all
too often downgrading rationality. By 'rationalistic' I
mean the outlook which says there is nothing worth
knowing that cannot be discerned purely by human
thought processes. That is certainly an outlook we need
to question. But to be rational simply means to use our
brains. Many New Agers have reacted against this in such
an extreme fashion that they will instinctively distrust
anything that seems to make logical ('left-brained')
sense. In his book *I am the Gate*, Bhagwan Shree
Rajneesh claims that thinking in an analytical, left-
brained fashion will actually prevent a person from
achieving spiritual enlightenment: 'It is not that the
intellect sometimes misunderstands. Rather, the intellect
always misunderstands. It is not that the intellect
sometimes errs; it is that the intellect is the error . . .'[4] As a
result, thousands of people assume that if something
seems to make sense by our normal definitions of logic, it
must automatically be suspect – and so they live their lives
on the basis of information supplied to them through
fairies and elves, dolphins and crystals, and techniques
such as self-hypnosis and channeling, while rejecting
out-of-hand the message of Jesus as recorded in the
Bible. The best that can be said, even on a charitable
assessment of it, is that these channeled messages are of
uncertain origin – and therefore cannot be tested or
authenticated in any meaningful sense. Yet they are
unconditionally believed and acted upon by people who
airily dismiss the Christian tradition as an unbelievable
hoax. A typical line is to claim that the Bible as we now
have it was concocted in the fourth century by nasty male
Church leaders in order to keep women in subjection, to

affirm their own domination and to get rid of inconvenient concepts like reincarnation that they disliked, but which were allegedly part of Christian belief at the very beginning. It is not uncommon to hear people claim that Jesus himself was some sort of channeler of extraterrestrial spirit guides. And it is taken for granted by all New Agers that the Jesus we read of in the New Testament is a con, and that the real Jesus is revealed in the various Gnostic gospels that circulated in the first two or three Christian centuries, but were later suppressed.

You don't need to be a card-carrying New Ager to think like this. Probably most people who ever give Jesus a second thought have come across such reasoning. It has certainly been adopted by the secular western media as their standard view, and has been heavily promoted in many popular books and TV programmes. I have already dealt with all this at considerable length in my 1989 book, *The Bible – Fact or Fantasy?*, so I will not engage in a detailed examination of it here. Except to say that it is all absolute rubbish. It bears no relationship to the facts, and people who believe it are simply deluding themselves. Of course New Agers would like to think Jesus taught reincarnation and was a channeler of spirit guides – because they do admire certain aspects of his teaching, and want to include him among the great Spiritual Masters of the ages. So the fact that the New Testament depicts him in a radically different way is a real problem. But it is both naive and dishonest to suppose that the problem can be overcome just by deciding that the Bible is not to be trusted. The Bible is our only useful source of information about Jesus, and if we are unable to trust that, then we can probably know nothing at all about Him. The fact that we may dislike what it says does not entitle us to discard its evidence as worthless. The New

Testament does make ultimate truth claims, and any useful spirituality needs to deal with that fact somewhere along the line.

This is only one example of the ways in which New Agers attempt to discredit Christianity. At other times, a one-sided view of history is put forward, in which Christians are believed to be the cause of the environmental crisis, or the instigators of all the world's war and injustice. No one could deny that Christians have often neglected the teaching of Jesus on these and other subjects, but to suggest this is the natural and inevitable outcome of following Jesus is misleading and mischievous. It simply draws attention to the fact that Christians frequently make wrong moral choices, like everyone else.

Along with all this, New Agers are quite happy to perpetuate their own mythologies quite uncritically. For example, it is taken for granted that division, confrontation and hard-headed rationality – all signs of the old Age of Pisces – are male characteristics, whereas harmony, peace, wholeness and spirituality are female characteristics – and these are what we need in the new Age of Aquarius. This then becomes another stick with which to beat any worldview that – however implausibly – might be labelled 'paternalistic', and is used to show, for example, that only worship of the earth goddess (Gaia) can save the planet. The desirability of these so-called 'female' qualities is not in question, but the idea that they have anything to do with gender simply cannot be supported. Anyone who lived through the Thatcher era in British politics would need to be gullible in the extreme to believe all that – and there are plenty of other historical examples which show that moral and social attitudes simply cannot be divided so neatly on the basis of gender.

In any case, what happens to concepts of equality and freedom if things are classified like this?

We could go on. The point is that many of the things which New Agers take for granted are simply untrue – and when these irrational statements are made as if they were true, we need to be prepared to stand up and put the record straight. Shirley Maclaine quotes the well-known channeler Kevin Ryerson asking, 'Did what came through *feel* right? They've told me to just trust my feelings. There's nothing else you can do once you begin to ask these questions.'[5] A few pages later she adds, 'The thing is it all seems to be about 'feeling', not thinking.'[6] There can be no question that western Christians have often ignored the relationship of faith to feelings. But feelings by themselves are unlikely to be any more useful than rationality by itself. Either way – by relying exclusively on one or the other – we are not whole people. While, on the one hand, we cannot understand everything by our own unaided efforts at rational analysis, we cannot, on the other hand, hide our heads in the sand and pretend that we are not rational people. We have brains, and to be fully human we need to use them.

THE SUPERNATURAL

But there are bigger challenges for the Church here – and the supernatural is one of the biggest. Just what do Christians really think about this? New Agers know with conviction that there is another world, another dimension of human existence, and to be in touch with it can give new meaning to life here and now. Spirit guides, extraterrestrial entities, mysterious healings, self-discovery – one way or another, just about everything in New Age thinking is related to belief in the supernatural. But where do Christians stand? Can we really put our hands on our hearts and say we believe in the supernatural and the miraculous? Mostly, the answer seems to be 'no.' I shall never forget a conversation I had with one of the world's leading New Agers. She had been brought up a Baptist, and had a shrewd understanding of the typical Christian mind-set. Explaining to me why, for her, the New Age Movement made more sense than the Church, she simply said, 'Frankly, the Church is full of rationalists. I know people who are Christians and who will fight tooth and nail to the last drop of their blood to defend the belief that Jesus performed miracles. And the same Christians will fight just as vociferously to deny that there is any such thing as the miraculous and the supernatural in our world today . . . The problem with you Christians is that you don't actually believe there is anything more than what can be seen, handled, felt and explained by the grey stuff in your left brain. But that just doesn't make sense to me.'

As a Christian, there was nothing I could say, for I knew this statement was right on the mark. She was describing the classic Reformed Evangelical position. Basically it is a rationalist viewpoint with an unexpected twist in it: the supernatural is all right, so long as we keep it in the past, and it doesn't relate to life here and now. The Church is going to have to face the fact that if we are serious about sharing our faith in Christ with people who are attracted to the New Age worldview, then our prevailing intellectually based, excessively cerebral form of the Christian faith will have to change. It will never meet the needs of people who are searching for spiritual reality as we move toward the twenty-first century.

This is probably our biggest challenge. For when New Agers claim that the Church is itself a part of the rationalist establishment mind-set that has sustained our modern world, then the facts are largely on their side. The new thinking of the European Enlightenment had a profound impact on the Christian Church, particularly on its understanding of the Bible. In a scientific climate dominated by the view that the only way to get at the real facts about anything was by the intellectual endeavour of thinking people, it seemed as if there was no real place for religion of any sort. Motivated by a heady mixture of rationalism and philosophical idealism, nineteenth-century thinkers were soon proclaiming that the Bible – far from being a revelation about God – contained only a mixture of history, ancient philosophy and mythology, none of which could stand up to critical scientific scrutiny.

Naturally, this created great alarm within the Church, and its best theological brains were forced to engage with this critical questioning. We have already identified Friedrich Schleiermacher as a major player in this drama, with his proposal to reclassify faith in such a way that it would be removed altogether from the realm of rational understanding. This certainly had the effect of rescuing Christianity from the immediate onslaughts of unbelieving rationalists. But what was left was a very vague, subjective collection of ideas, and this separation of religious faith from facts ultimately led to the kind of Christianity that dominates the western Church today. Schleiermacher was not the only actor in this philosophical drama, of course. Well into the twentieth century, the same questions were being addressed by Christian thinkers – most notably, perhaps, by the German theologian Rudolf Bultmann. He eventually concluded that we can know next to nothing about the historical Jesus, but argued that faith doesn't need that kind of rational certainty anyway. How ironic that the well-intentioned efforts of people like this to rescue

Christianity from secular rationalism have led to the emergence of a form of Christianity that has itself become so rationalistic that it is apparently unable to meet the spiritual needs of today's people! And it is ironic, too, that at the very time when Bultmann was vigorously promoting the 'demythologizing' of the Bible, new discoveries in the natural sciences were forcing other people to remythologize their entire understanding of how the world is!

It is an irony that has produced whole generations of Church leaders who understand their own faith heritage in reductionist terms, and who regard spiritual experience as little more than a branch of social anthropology. Nor is this a malady that afflicts only one section of the Church. For at the opposite end of the theological spectrum to Bultmann, the same basic worldview produces Fundamentalist preachers who regularly confuse knowledge of God with knowledge of Bible texts. They can answer every question you ever thought of – and a good deal more besides – but are spiritually powerless either to change themselves or to channel blessing into the lives of others. The scandals that have bedevilled American tele-evangelists in recent years are evidence of this powerlessness.

Historically, western Christians have simply not believed in the supernatural. Today I sense an even more devious way of thinking coming into some of our churches. Many are now quite happy to say they believe in some sort of spiritual or supernatural dimension of faith, but nevertheless remain fundamentally closed to it. They say they believe in gifts of the Spirit, but somehow never get round to exercising any of them. They say they believe in healing and wholeness, but never create space for it to happen in the regular life of their congregations.

Of couse, I recognize all the questions that modern western clergy have about subjects such as this, and I would not for a moment wish to play down their relevance. This is not the place to rehearse them. But the fact is that Christians with an essentially non-supernatural faith will make little progress with today's spiritual pilgrims in the New Age Movement. If Christians question, for example, the existence of guardian angels, should we really be surprised that people put spirit guides in their place? If we deny the healing power of Christ, what is more natural than for people to turn elsewhere – to crystal power? And if we are incapable of channeling the affirming love and peace of Christ into the lives of others, how can we be surprised if they turn instead to the techniques of transpersonal psychology? As C. S. Lewis once put it, 'It is since Christians have largely ceased to think of the other world that they have become so ineffective in this.'

BECOMING WHOLE PERSONS

Words like 'holistic' (or is it 'wholistic?') are part of the regular jargon of the New Age Movement, and the yearning for wholeness – however we spell it – is one of the most widely felt human needs today. People feel disjointed, out of tune with their physical environment, out of touch with other people, and even unable to come to terms with themselves. There is a lot of hurt around, and there are many wounded people who are looking for personal healing. To be relevant to life in the next millenium, any religious faith will have to be capable of dealing effectively with such feelings of alienation and lostness.

This should hardly be a challenge for the Christian

message. Jesus himself offered to make people whole, and throughout his teaching he described a life of fulfilment in which the divisions that cause pain can be healed. A holistic lifestyle features strongly in the pages of the New Testament. It is God's will. Yet the Christian Church is one of the most striking examples not of wholeness, but of separation. This is most obviously seen in the mere fact that the Church itself is so divided. One of the most pathetic images from the TV coverage of the 1991 Gulf War was of British soldiers standing in the desert celebrating the Eucharist, with two tables set up alongside each other: one for Protestants, the other for Roman Catholics. They could live – and die – together, but not worship together! Church leaders delude themselves if they think this sort of thing commends the Christian faith to genuine searchers after the life of the spirit. It only serves to reinforce the negative and destructive image that the Church already has for most people in the West today.

But there is an even more insidious problem to be faced, namely the closet Christianity that has become the norm for so many throughout all denominations. The phenomenon is well known and hardly needs to be documented. Even for Church members, faith in Christ can be an optional extra. At church on Sunday mornings they wear it like a garment, then they go home and hang it up in the closet for the rest of the week. They live their lives and choose their everyday values with absolutely no reference whatever to what they say they believe. Again, this is all so contrary to the teaching of Jesus and the lifestyles of the first Christians. Their faith was nothing if not holistic: it applied to the whole of life, and no part of the human personality, no experience, was excluded from the transforming power of Christ's Spirit.

If our message cannot lead people into a new dimension of personal development and maturity, and enable them to understand themselves as they discover new ways of relating to God, then why should we expect anyone to be interested in it? Asking why so many people today are gravitating towards divination, shamanism, altered states of consciousness, and other spiritual practices, Robert Bellah, a sociologist at the University of California at Berkeley, puts his finger on our problem. 'Mainline Churches are bland,' he says; 'people want something more interesting – like channeling or getting in touch with spirits.'[7] I would personally question whether too many people are quite so desperate to get in touch with spirit guides, though an increasing number are. But I know for certain that many more are uneasy about the shallow relationships and glib advice they get from the Churches.

Shirley Maclaine identifies the same sense of searching for a deeper reality when she describes a UK politician with whom she once had a relationship. In writing of this man whom she calls Gerry, she says:

He travelled through Africa as a young man. But when he spoke of it, I suddenly realized that he never once mentioned what he ate, what he touched, what he saw, what he smelled, how he felt. He spoke mainly about Africa as a sociological trip, not as a human trip. He spoke of how the 'masses' were exploited and poor and colonised, but never how they really lived and felt about it.[8]

Change the language a little, and you get a good description of how many Christians think of and describe God – as a sociological (theological) trip, not as a human trip. This is the inevitable consequence of the way

Christian theology – both liberal and conservative – has allowed rationalism to evacuate it of any sense of direct encounter with God. A lot of people would readily identify with Ian Wray when he complains that Christianity is dominated by 'dwelling intellectually upon the dogma, with a consequent lack of therapeutic, by which I mean the lack of any real body of ideas and practices to help people change'.[9] This deficiency has clearly been a key factor in the rising popularity of New Age therapies. Wray goes on: '. . . the near total absence of practical aids to human psychological and spiritual growth within Christianity left a vacuum which psychotherapy had to fill, based upon principles which it had to discover for itself.'

It is hardly surprising, then, that what has rushed in to fill the void is not based on a Christian worldview, but on the philosophy of positive thinking, in which ultimately 'man is the measure of all things', and there is no room for a God who is beyond and above and different from us. The New Testament demand, 'Love your neighbour as yourself' has been rephrased to read, 'Love God as yourself' – something that is easy enough to do, if you yourself are 'God'.

Like many ideas floating around in the New Age Movement the view that 'You are what you make yourself' does, of course, have a degree of truth in it. If you have a low self-image, then you are always likely to find yourself at the bottom of the pile. Conversely, a degree of self-confidence can make you a different person. Historically, some Christian traditions have utilized this fact to give their members a low self-esteem. Living as I do in Scotland, which is a predominantly presbyterian and calvinist culture, I regularly meet people whose only legacy from the Church is a massive burden of guilt and feelings of personal worthlessness. They can testify at first hand to the destructive force of such an outlook. I have myself heard literally hundreds of sermons which have had a good deal more to say about sin than about forgiveness, or Christ's love, or spiritual power. The answer to this is not to ignore or play down the reality of evil in our world. That is what the New Age Movement does, and it leads to the kind of moral weakness that has been noted in previous chapters. But we must recognize that themes such as 'original sin' and 'total depravity' (which in any case have more to do with Augustine than with the New Testament) have all too often been used to put people down and evacuate them of self-worth.

Michael Anast, of California's Foundation for Spiritual Freedom, complains that 'Old line religions hold people down from being who they are'[10] – and there is no denying that churches have often done exactly that. But contrast this with Jesus, who was the exact opposite. He always lifted people up and affirmed them. People who met him always felt better as a result of their encounter. Except for one or two, that is. It has to be significant that the only people Jesus ever put down were the religious and self-righteous. We have much to learn from his attitude. If *he* could take evil seriously, without humiliating people, why can his twentieth-century followers not do the same? I remember once asking a class of university students to draw a sketch of what came into their mind when they heard the word 'evangelist'. There were several predictable cartoons – of priests in pulpits and preachers on soap boxes at street corners, and so on. But one drew a striking caricature of the film character Rambo! His sole purpose in life is to annihilate the opposition. Jesus was no Rambo. But too many Christians are like Rambo, and too few are like Jesus. We need to apply Jesus' example not only to evangelism, but also to Church organization. Real leaders should be open to other people and their needs; they should not be mere power-brokers running an impersonal corporation.

That is not the only reason why we have little to say to people who are genuinely searching for personal spiritual and psychological fulfilment in life. There are also some quite specific parts of Jesus' teaching whose significance we seem to have missed – such as his commandment in Mark 12: 'You shall love the Lord your God with all your heart, with all your soul, with all your mind, and with all your strength.' Because of our inbuilt bias towards thinking, we have missed the fact that Jesus identified thinking as only one-fourth of our total response to God. For as well as our minds, he instructs us to use our hearts (emotions), our souls (spirits) and our strength (bodies) to express our love for God. Discovering ways of doing that can be a very liberating experience. Not everybody out there is cerebrally organized. H. G. Wells once claimed, 'Most people think once or twice in a lifetime. I've made a reputation of thinking once or twice a month.' Most of us make our major life decisions not through being intellectually convinced about what we should do, but on the basis of our feelings and intuitions. When you fall in love, you're not too concerned about 'facts' such as your partner's hair colour or height, or even his or her age. How you feel about each other is far more important than any of these things, and will ultimately determine the course of the relationship. Knowing another person involves an intimate bond that is rooted in the emotions and the body, with the mind usually coming in a poor third. How strange, then, that Christians find it so easy to talk of God in personal terms, but so difficult to relate to God on any but a cerebral, theological level. Is this why the Church is so unattractive to so many people today? Could it be that our failure to appeal to the masses in the western world is not, as many suppose, a matter of social class, but one of lifestyles and perspectives? If you major exclusively on thinking things through intellectually, then you are bound to attract a certain sort of bookish person. But there are fewer and fewer – even among the middle class, the traditional supporters of the Church – who now believe that the world's problems are going to be solved by our own unaided reason.

SPIRITUAL THERAPIES

If we only diagnose people's problems, without offering effective solutions, we are playing a very dangerous psychological and spiritual game. 'Effective' is the key word here, for theologically, solutions are usually offered. But leaving people knowing only in a theoretical sort of way that there is an escape from guilt and failure is not going to be of much practical assistance, if you then have to access it yourself without really knowing what is being recommended or required.

Western preachers are adept at analyzing and defining the challenges that face people, but frequently they leave it at that. It is as if a great barrier comes crashing down at the very point where people most need some help – the place where theory needs to lead to action. Why do so many of us back off from leading people into practical spirituality, apparently fearing that some great wave of uncontrollable emotionalism will come breaking over our congregations? The sad truth is that most Christians have their emotional lids so firmly screwed down that there is absolutely no chance of that. We have never learned how to love Christ with anything but our minds.

Unless our emotions and our bodies can engage with

our spirituality, we are missing something very special. I know that westerners – the British in particular, being very private people – like to keep their spiritual commitments under wraps if they can possibly manage it. But I wonder if leaving people to work it all out for themselves – just you and God in a secret place – is really the Gospel of Jesus Christ. Is it not a subtle adaptation of the essentially secular gospel of western individualism – the spiritual equivalent of the economic exhortation to 'stand on your own two feet'? If the Holy Spirit offers us the power to be different people – as the New Testament states clearly on every page – then the next question is, How do I access that power? For that we need rather more than theological statements, however true they might be. We need spiritual disciplines, techniques and practices that will lead us somewhere, that will facilitate us in relation to ourselves as we consciously and deliberately open our lives to God's supernatural power, in order to effect radical change.

When we look to our Christian heritage, there is a whole rich tradition of such things that have been marginalized and largely ignored in the modern Church. Now the New Agers have come along and have begun to ransack them for their own purposes. As I have begun to reclaim some of this in my own ministry, I have been truly amazed at the powerful way in which God can work in people's lives through the simplest of methodologies. I recall a large evangelical church, where my wife and I led an extended series of workshops on spirituality. These people knew so much theology it was coming out of their ears. There wasn't a question to which they didn't know the answer. But they had never really applied their theology to their emotions and their bodies, both of which remained fundamentally uncommitted to Christ. These

Christians had never been exposed to the Gospel in a way that could challenge them in these dimensions of existence. As we began to express our love for Christ through the medium of dance and physical movement, I knew this was going to be a special series of workshops. But I was still not prepared for what was to happen when we introduced creative imagery. Using our imaginations (part of our God-given equipment), we saw ourselves as we were, and as we would like to be – and then visualized Christ moving in to remodel us. Within less than half a minute, many of these people – both men and women – were discovering God in new and dramatic ways, and were absolutely overwhelmed as they began to experience the love of Christ pouring into their lives in an almost physically discernible torrent. It was as if one of the great promises of the New Testament instantaneously began to take shape before our very eyes: 'we shall all come together in that oneness in our faith and in our knowledge of the Son of God; we shall become mature people, reaching to the very height of Christ's full stature' (Ephesians 4:13). These people knew all about the personal wholeness promised by Christ – in theory. But it took more than mere head knowledge for something to begin to happen, and for wholeness to become a reality in their lives.

I learned something else in that church too. For not everyone present at those workshops was a Christian. An overseas visitor was also there. He was certainly interested in the Christian faith and, as he told me later, he had been intellectually convinced by it for some time – but he was not committed to Christ. For that, his body and his emotions needed to be opened up to the reality of God's love. And they were – as we danced, but especially as we looked into an imaginary mirror, seeing ourselves through God's eyes, hearing God's voice telling us of our true value, and imagining God stepping inside to remake us in the image of Christ. We could have shared the Gospel only in words that night – and that man would have gone away as he came. What he needed was someone to facilitate him in expressing his embryonic love for Christ – and for him, guided imagery was the key that unlocked the door.

Now some western Christians will say that the use of creative imagery is itself New Age, and even satanic. This is a defensive response which certainly owes more to secular rationalism than it does to the message of Jesus, for it effectively denies what Jesus commended when he spoke of loving God with all your heart, soul, mind and strength. It also puts a question mark against some of Jesus' own spiritual experience. He once told his disciples 'I saw Satan fall like lightning from heaven'; at another time he reported having rebuked Satan on numerous occasions; and after his resurrection he spoke with the couple on the road to Emmaus, and quite clearly invoked their imaginative capacities. Paul too had experiences that, if they happened today, would easily be labelled 'New Age' – including, apparently, out-of-body experiences (2 Corinthians 12:1–6). In our understandable enthusiasm to challenge the New Age worldview, we must beware of becoming paranoid about such things. Creative visualization has always been one of the key elements in African-American preaching, and no doubt that explains why so many people have found the sermons of preachers like Martin Luther King so moving – because they have been involved themselves, as more than mere listeners. The fact that a New Ager finds a particular therapy or technique helpful does not in itself brand it as New Age in the technical sense, and therefore problematical for a Christian. Remember the description of the New Age as a vacuum cleaner? New Agers suck up all sorts of things from many diverse sources, just because they find them useful – including lots of things from Christian sources. A catalogue of New Age music tapes lying on my desk just now advertises Gregorian chants and the music of Graham Kendrick played on the Spanish guitar, as well as more obviously New Age offerings!

I had a vivid reminder of the eclectic character of the New Age even as I was writing this chapter. For I write in the middle of a Scottish winter, and I have been spending much of my free time on the ski slopes. Going up to the top of the *piste* one day, I started a conversation with the person with whom I was sharing the T-bar tow. He immediately told me he was a New Ager, and that skiing is now a major New Age pursuit that has the power to break the barriers between the right brain and the left and give access to new dimensions of self-understanding. On top of that, there is the added bonus that, since skiing takes you out into the wild, it brings you closer to Gaia, the earth goddess! Anyone who has experienced the exhilaration of skiing down a mountainside at eighty kilometres per hour will know exactly what he meant. It certainly gives you new insights into yourself. Watching the red glow of a winter sun sinking over the snow-clad peaks could easily register as a spiritual experience for most people. Should I then give up my favourite winter sport, just because a New Ager can interpret it like this? Of course not. Skiing itself is spiritually neutral, and we can all see that. The same is also true of something like creative imagery. Of course, not all imagining is good and healthy: a young woman can have such a distorted image of herself as being overweight that she becomes anorexic.

In using such techniques, the crucial thing is the object on which we fix our imagination. For the New Ager, creative visualization centres on myself as the answer to every problem, and assures me that my own will or Higher Self is the key to effecting personal change. But as a Christian, I centre not on myself but on Christ, recognizing that I myself cannot effect lasting and radical change, and that I need God to come in and transform things.

Christians ignore spiritual disciplines like this at their peril. If we only feed our minds, we will become spiritually deformed and disabled – and as a result, those who know they need some transforming experience will look elsewhere. Many people are drawn to the New Age Movement not particularly because they share its overall worldview, but because it appears to hold out the promise of enabling them to become better people. People need something tangible through which to express their deepest life commitments. Ideas are fine. Thinking is fine. I've spent most of my adult life thinking about religion, so I'm the last person to underestimate the value of theological statements. But thinking – even about theology – does not change lives. The Bible itself makes it abundantly clear that mere knowledge of facts is not enough. The gospels are full of stories about people who saw the facts, but, because of their perceptions, missed the real point of it all. While the Pharisees debated on an intellectual level about messianic theology, the poor and the marginalized experienced the miraculous power of Jesus. And while the Pharisees wondered if he could be John the Baptist, Elijah or whoever, only Peter saw that he was 'the Christ of God'. What was the difference? A faith-inspired use of the imagination that enabled Peter and the other believers to experience a real paradigm shift in their whole way of seeing things. We should never forget that God came into our world not as a book of theology, but as a person. That, whatever else it implies, must certainly mean that authentic Christianity will always be person-centred, and never book-centred.

GROWING TOGETHER

Personal commitment to God implies commitment to other people. Or does it? Here is another radical challenge that New Age thinking is presenting to the Church. In a previous chapter, we looked at some of the ways in which the New Age has broken into the world of corporate management training. The Church is one of the largest corporate organizations in the western world. Unfortunately, Church structures have developed very much along the lines of what Russell Ackoff so vividly describes as the outmoded and useless models of the Machine Age, in which

> . . . employees were treated as replaceable machines or machine parts even though they were known to be human beings. Their personal objectives . . . were considered irrelevant by employers . . . the very simple repetitive tasks they were given to do were designed as though they were to be performed by machines.[11]

Change the terminology a bit, and the description could easily be applied to almost any typical congregation of any major Christian denomination. There must be thousands of local churches where the members are but cogs in an ecclesiastical machine run by other people. One of the most extraordinary features of the contemporary Christian scene in Britain and America is the number of Christian people who are ecclesiastically homeless.

Hordes of them float around from one church to another, finding no deep acceptance anywhere, and consequently putting down no deep roots. At one time, such people could justly have been characterized as backsliders and renegades. But no longer, for most of them are deeply committed to Christ – a commitment that leads them to ask awkward questions that shock the establishment, as a result of which they can be deliberately marginalized, and frequently suffer deep personal hurt.

The uncomfortable truth is that here, as elsewhere, the Church has been all too eager to adopt the secular standards and practices of our prevailing western culture. As a result, when people look at us, they just see more of the hierarchies and bureaucracies that they experience elsewhere, and they know that this is not what will bring them personal spiritual fulfilment. If they go off to read the New Testament to discover Christ's will for the Church, they find there many statements about how the Church as the body of Christ should help them in their search for personal maturity and spiritual wholeness. Jesus himself said that the love of his disciples for one another should be a powerful magnet to attract other people. And so it would be for today's spiritual searchers. When management consultants and others talk of the need for interactive human structures in which people are given the space to grow and develop to their full potential, they are searching for something that the New Testament promises. Ackoff counsels that 'What is required is that individuals be able to evaluate their own quality of life, that they have an opportunity to improve it, that they be encouraged to do so, and that their efforts to do so be facilitated' – something he believes can be brought about 'by encouraging and facilitating the participation of the others in the design of and planning for the organizations and institutions of which they are a part'.[12] Where do we find such an organization? Christians, of all people, should know the answer to that. For what the New Testament says about the Church as the body of Christ is a perfect model of the kind of holistic systems that so many people are desperately searching for. The church should be a place where we can be accepted as we are – children, women and men together – a safe environment in which to discover more about ourselves, to experience personal growth and to make a contribution to the growth of others. When so very few of our congregations even begin to approximate to that ideal, need we be surprised that honest people look elsewhere?

LOOKING TO THE FUTURE

The forces represented by the New Age 'represent the single greatest opportunity and the single greatest threat the church of Christ has faced since apostolic times'.[13] Or so Os Guinness claimed in a striking address to the 1989 Lausanne II International Congress on World Evangelization. Like all effective communicators, he was exaggerating a little to drive his point home, but he was fundamentally right. At the same time, we should acknowledge that some aspects of Christian life deserve to be threatened. For we ourselves have gullibly accepted norms and standards that are totally inconsistent with the demands of the Gospel. When New Age thinking exposes our own secular rationalism, we must be prepared to take radical action. We should not under-estimate the extent to which the questions raised in this chapter will threaten the existing mind-set of Christians right across the theological and denominational spectrum today. But that is not the only threat we face. Nor, in the long run, is it the most menacing.

As the British TSB Bank said in its *TS Beat* Magazine back in 1990, 'New Age is good, is right and ready for now.'[14] The New Age Movement is tuning in to the legitimate concerns that people have as we stand on the threshold of a new millenium; it is addressing itself to widely felt human needs, and providing answers that sound plausible. At root, those answers are based on a worldview that is fundamentally opposed to Christianity, but which could easily become the dominant outlook of the next century. That must be the major threat facing the Christian Church. And unless we ourselves are prepared to change, it will be impossible to deal with. Something like four out of five of all New Agers I have ever met have at some time in their lives been part of the Church, and have left it. They discovered that their spiritual needs were not being satisfied by the churches with which they were involved. Nor is this a comment on any particular form of church. The New Agers I have met have come from many different Church traditions. They used to be Catholics, Protestants, Liberals, Fundamentalists, Charismatics and Reformed church members. Throughout the western world, the Church is losing ground and apparently has little to say to today's people. However uncomfortable it may be, we have to face up to the fact that people will not be brought to faith in Christ by what we are doing now. We no longer have the excuse that people today are secular and therefore not spiritually aware. They are more open to the spiritual than at any time this century. So why is it that when people need healing – whether personal, emotional or physical – they search for alternative therapies? Why is it that when they have a need to belong to a meaningful community the church is the last place they think of? Why is it that when they're looking for ministry to their emotions they go into altered states of consciousness? Why is it that when they want somebody to stand alongside them, to touch them, and to affirm them in some physical, bodily kind of way, they steer clear of Christians? We seem to be forced to the disagreeable and painful conclusion that they are not coming to Christ precisely because of what we are now doing in the Church.

But why is the New Age a great opportunity? Simply because never before in modern times have so many people been so aware of spiritual realities. Rapidly increasing numbers are finding it possible to believe in reincarnation, spirit guides and extraterrestrials, and all sorts of other esoteric ideas. To traditional Christians, this might be unfamiliar and threatening territory. But it certainly means that these people are spiritually open as no other generation within living memory has been. All New Agers are winnable for Christ. In the case of every New Ager I have ever met, I have felt that God could give that person to the Church as a gift, if only he or she could meet Christians in whose lives the reality of Christ was an everyday experience.

As we move into the twenty-first century and into a new millenium what kind of outlook will become the western worldview? There are only two possible contenders. One is the scientific materialist worldview that has dominated for the past two or three hundred years. That is already in a state of terminal decline. It may well not endure the remaining years of this century. It certainly has no chance of surviving for long into the next. The collapse of materialist atheism in eastern Europe is just the final nail in the coffin of the humanistic,

rationalist philosophy that has influenced us all for so
long. The decline of traditional mainstream Christianity
in Europe and North America – which has been but a
religious version of the same essentially rationalistic
outlook – only serves to reinforce that impression.

The other alternative is a supernatural worldview.
Something like the New Age mixture, perhaps. Indeed,
unless there is some dramatic change of direction, it is
likely that this will be embraced by more and more
western people. But despite its stated global concerns,
the New Age is essentially a western phenomenon. In
world terms, another scenario is possible. For though
western rationalist Christianity has been rejected, the
vast majority of the world's Christians are no longer
western, or indeed, white – and certainly not rationalists.
Is it merely coincidental that today's New Agers are
desperately looking to people who are non-western to
find the answer to our predicament, and that at exactly
this point in time the churches in the two-thirds world are
growing so fast? In Africa, south-east Asia, China, South
America – wherever we look, Christians who will frankly
challenge our own western views are mobilizing in vast
numbers and are making a significant impact in their own
cultures. Could it be that this will be the source from
which our bankrupt western theologies may yet under
God's providence find new direction for the twenty-first
century?

Make no mistake about it, these Christians are not
carbon copies of me or you. In the last few years I have
been greatly privileged to travel extensively all over the
world. I have met with Christian leaders from every
continent, and the stories I hear bear a remarkable
similarity to one another. From all parts of the mainline
churches and from all over the world, the story is the

same. There is an amazing growth of the Christian faith which is firmly linked to belief in the supernatural power of God. A high profile is given to healings, exorcisms, personal self-discovery and new forms of structural organization – all things that New Agers in the West are searching for. Direct, hands-on spiritual experience is high on the agenda of the world church.

It will not be easy for white, western Christians to learn from these people. For we still have our vestiges of imperialism. Not now a political imperialism, but certainly an intellectual imperialism that tries to rationalize what is happening in other places, and still claims that the way western people have traditionally understood the world is the only possible way that makes sense. What we are seeing today is the emergence of a new way of thinking about God, that is radically different from traditional western theology, accompanied by a new confidence in direct personal experience of God that is quite unlike anything we know in the West. To characterize this as 'charismatic' is misleading, for it is happening in mainstream churches and is in many respects different from the western charismatic movement, which is still basically locked into a scholastic and rationalist way of thinking.

One way or another, the western Church is in for a traumatic time ahead. The year 2000 will soon be upon us. New hopes and aspirations are rising fast, and all over the world people have a renewed expectancy that we are about to enter a new era. Whether with capital letters or not, a 'new age' is about to dawn. Charting a new course will not be easy. But it will certainly be exciting. New Agers are reminding us that we cannot face the future without also coming to terms with the past. We western Christians need to face the immediate past. As we reflect on the last two or three centuries we will find much for which we need to repent. Christians in the two-thirds world are also directing us to the more distant past, as Jesus is rediscovered for the twenty-first century. For the rapid growth of the Church throughout the world today is largely a rediscovery of this unique figure. When Jesus is stripped of the misunderstandings we have imposed on him, his teaching and his person speak in a unique way to the spiritual aspirations of the world's people. And if we Christians get our act together that can also include those who are presently caught up in the New Age Movement. When the Church of Christ more adequately begins to reflect the love of Christ, we can confidently expect more of today's spiritual pilgrims to affirm, for, in the words of the closing eucharistic prayer in the 1982 Scottish liturgy, 'Jesus is *Lord of all ages*, world without end'.

NOTES

NOTES

No sources are given for statements taken from personal interviews.

CHAPTER 1

1. Joanna Lumley, quoted in *Woman's Weekly*, 9 October 1990, p. 26.
2. Robert Ellwood, interview with *The Philadelphia Inquirer*, 7 January 1990.
3. Kenny Kaufman, quoted in *San Francisco Chronicle*, 25 April 1990.
4. Hemitra Crecraft & Sue King, interview with *The Philadelphia Inquirer*, 7 January 1990.
5. Shirley Maclaine, *Out on a Limb* (Bantam Books, London, 1987), p. 140.
6. Carol Riddell, *The Findhorn Community* (Findhorn Press, Findhorn, 1991), p. 64.
7. Shirley Maclaine, op. cit., pp. 327–8.
8. John Carman, quoted in *San Francisco Chronicle*, 28 April 1988.
9. *TS Beat*, Issue 9 (1990), pp. 6–7.

10. Korra Deaver, *Rock Crystal: the Magic Stone* (Samuel Weiser, York Beach, Maine, 1985), p. 40.
11. Marilyn Ferguson, *The Aquarian Conspiracy* (J. P. Tarcher, Los Angeles, 1980), pp. 111–12.
12. Kenneth Wapnick, *Forgiveness & Jesus* (Foundation for A Course in Miracles, Roscoe, NY, 1983), p. 318.

CHAPTER 2

1. 'The members speak: what does "New Age" mean to you?', *New Age Journal*, November–December 1987, p. 52.
2. *San Francisco Chronicle*, 8 July 1990, p. 8.
3. Sir George Trevelyan, 'Spiritual Awakening in our Time' in W. Bloom (ed.), *The New Age: an anthology of essential writings* (Rider Publications, London, 1991), p. 33.
4. William Irwin Thompson, *From Nation to Emancipation* (Findhorn Publications, Findhorn, 1982), p. 52.
5. Jose Arguelles, 'Harmonic Convergence, Trigger event: implementation and follow-up', *Life Times Magazine*, No. 3, p. 65.
6. Zbigniew Brzezinski, interview in *New York Times*, 31 December 1978.
7. Fritjof Capra, *The Turning Point* (Flamingo, London, 1983), p. xvii.
8. Marilyn Ferguson, *The Aquarian Conspiracy*, op. cit., pp. 125, 142.

CHAPTER 3

1. Shirley Maclaine, *Out on a Limb*, op. cit., p. 215.
2. Ibid., p. 198.
3. Marilyn Ferguson, *The Aquarian Conspiracy*, pp. 380.

4. Russell L. Ackoff, *Creating the Corporate Future* (John Wiley & Sons, New York, 1981), p. 19.
5. R. Scott Peck, *The Road Less Traveled* (Simon & Schuster, New York, 1978), pp. 281, 283.
6. *Bhagavad Gita* 2:46.
7. Michael Murphy & Rhea A. White, *The Psychic Side of Sports* (Addison-Wesley, Reading, Mass., 1978), pp. 5–6.
8. Marilyn Ferguson, op. cit., p. 101.
9. *The Gospel of Thomas*, logion 77.

CHAPTER 4

1. B. McWaters, *Conscious Evolution* (New Age Press, Los Angeles, 1981), pp. 111–12.
2. Shirley Maclaine, *Out on a Limb*, p. 209.
3. Ibid., p. 187.
4. J. White, 'Channeling, a short history of a long tradition', in *Holistic Life Magazine*, Summer, 1985, p. 22.
5. M. J. Crowe, *The Extraterrestrial Life Debate 1750–1900* (Cambridge University Press, London, 1988), p. 547.
6. J. Z. Knight, *A State of Mind* (Warner Books, New York, 1987), pp. 11–12.
7. Shirley Maclaine, op. cit., p. 136.
8. J. L. Simmons, *The Emerging New Age* (Bear & Co., Santa Fe, 1990), pp. 69–70.
9. Ibid., p. 83.
10. C. S. Lewis, *The Screwtape Letters* (Macmillan, New York, 1943), pp. 32–33.
11. J. L. Simmons, op. cit., p. 95.
12. Carol Zaleski, *Other World Journeys* (Oxford University Press, New York, 1987), p. 205.

13. J. L. Simmons, op. cit., p. 117.
14. R. C. Zaehner, *Our Savage God: the perverse use of eastern thought* (Sheed & Ward, New York, 1974), pp. 71–72.
15. Richard Smoley, 'Fundamental Differences', in *Gnosis* 14 (Winter 1990), p. 50.
16. J. L. Simmons, op. cit., p. 61.
17. Robert Monroe, *Journeys out of the Body* (Anchor Books, Garden City, NY, 1973), references to pp. 138–139.
18. J. L. Simmons, op. cit., p. 78.
19. Alice Bailey, *The Problems of Humanity* (Lucifer Press, London, 1947), quotations from pp. 115–27.
20. David Spangler, *Revelation: the birth of a New Age* (Findhorn Publications, Findhorn, 1976), references to pp. 10–11.
21. Margaret Brearley, 'Matthew Fox: Creation Spirituality for the Aquarian Age' in *Christian-Jewish Relations* 22 (1989), p. 48.

CHAPTER 5

1. Marilyn Ferguson, *The Aquarian Conspiracy*, p. 267.
2. Shirley Maclaine, *Dancing in the Light* (Bantam Books, New York, 1985), p. 8.
3. Jill Ireland, *Life Wish* (Little, Brown & Co., Boston, 1987), p. 77.
4. R. C. Fuller, *Alternative Medicine and American Religious Life* (Oxford University Press, New York, 1989), pp. 119–20 *(italics mine)*.
5. George Bush, *Mesmer and Swedenborg* (John Allen, New York, 1847), p. 160.

6. A. T. Still, *Autobiography of Andrew T. Still* (Kirksville, Mo., 1897), p. 99.
7. A. T. Still in *Journal of Osteopathy*, May 1894, p. 1.
8. R. W. Trine, *In Tune with the Infinite* (Thomas Crowell, New York, 1897), p. 16.
9. J. H. Kellogg, *The Living Temple* (Good Health Publishing Co., Battle Creek, 1903), p. 40.
10. P. P. Quimby, *The Quimby Manuscripts* (Thomas Crowell, New York, 1921), pp. 180, 319, 173.
11. S. C. Hahnemann, *Organon of the Rational Art of Healing* (E. P. Dutton, New York, 1913), p. 102.
12. A. Fritsche, *Hahnemann, Die Ideem der Homoeopathie* (Berlin, 1944), pp. 263, 264.
13. D. D. Palmer, *The Chiropractor's Adjustor* (Portland Printing House, Portland, Ore., 1910), p. 821.
14. B. J. Palmer, *Do Chiropractors Pray?* (Palmer School of Chiropractic, Davenport, Iowa, 1911), p. 25.
15. G. F. Reikman, 'Chiropractic' in *The Holistic Health Handbook* (And/Or Press, Berkeley, 1978), pp. 171–4.
16. *The Holistic Health Handbook*, p. 17.
17. Alice Bailey, 'Esoteric Healing' in *The New Age: an anthology of essential writings*, p. 88.
18. J. Keel, *The Eighth Tower* (Signet Books, New York, 1975), p. 16.
19. Korra Deaver, *Rock Crystal: the Magic Stone*, p. 36.
20. S. Thomson, *Boston Thomsonian Manual* 3 (15 November 1837), p. 21.
21. D. Kreiger, *The Therapeutic Touch* (Prentice-Hall, Englewood Cliffs, NJ, 1979), p. 13.
22. R. C. Fuller, op. cit., p. 99.
23. Karol Sikora, interview in the London *Evening Standard*, 14 January 1991.

24. J. L. Simmons, *The Emerging New Age*, pp. 158–9.
25. C. Myss, 'Redefining the healing process' in *The New Age: an anthology of essential writings*, pp. 86–7.
26. J. L. Simmons, op. cit., p. 79.
27. Marilyn Ferguson, op. cit., pp. 253–4.
28. L. Fallowfield, quoted in the London *Evening Standard*, 14 January 1991.
29. A. & O. Worrall, *The Miracle Healers* (Signet Books, New York, 1969).
30. John Harris, *New Age: a Christian response to a serious challenge* (Zadok Institute, Barton, ACT, 1991), p. 5.
31. J. L. Simmons, op. cit., p. 161.
32. Editorial in *Watercure Journal* (12) 1852, p. 12.
33. M. Duke, *Acupuncture* (Pyramid House, New York, 1972), p. 164.
34. Dorothy Maclean, quoted in Paul Hawken, *The Magic of Findhorn* (Fontana, London, 1988), p. 146.
35. Terence McKenna, quoted in *San Francisco Chronicle*, 25 April 1990.
36. Richard Smoley, 'Fundamental Differences', in *Gnosis* 14 (winter 1990), pp. 50–1.

CHAPTER 6

1. Russell Ackoff, *Creating the Corporate Future*, p. 13.
2. Ackoff, op. cit., p. 13.
3. Ackoff, op. cit., pp. 25–6.
4. Ackoff, op. cit., pp. 19–20.
5. Ackoff, op. cit., p. 19.
6. Ackoff, op. cit., p. 34.
7. Ackoff, op. cit., p. 6.

8. Jack Underhill, 'New Age Quiz', in *Life Times Magazine* no. 3, p. 6.
9. M. Ferguson, *The Aquarian Conspiracy*, p. 24.
10. M. Ferguson, op. cit., p. 352.
11. M. Ferguson, op. cit., p. 118.
12. William H. Kautz & Melanie Branon, *Channeling: the Intuitive Connection* (Harper & Row, San Francisco, 1987), pp. 136–7.

CHAPTER 7

1. *The San Francisco Chronicle* poll was published in the editions for 24 & 25 April 1990.
2. Marilyn Ferguson, *The Aquarian Conspiracy*, p. 85.
3. James Sire, *Scripture Twisting* (Inter-Varsity Press, Downers Grove, Ill., 1980), p. 18.
4. B. S. Rajneesh, *I am the Gate* (Harper & Row, New York, 1977), p. 18.
5. Shirley Maclaine, *Out on a Limb*, p. 210.
6. Ibid., p. 215.
7. Robert Bellah, quoted in *San Francisco Chronicle*, 25 April 1990.
8. Shirley Maclaine, op. cit., p. 41.
9. I. Wray, 'Buddhism and Psychotherapy' in G. Claxton, *Beyond Therapy* (Wisdom Publications, London, 1986), pp. 160–1.
10. Michael Anast, interview with *San Francisco Chronicle*, 1 December 1989.
11. Russell Ackoff, *Creating the Corporate Future*, p. 26.
12. Ibid., p. 44.

13. Os Guinness, 'The impact of modernization' in J. D. Douglas, *Proclaim Christ until He Comes* (Worldwide Publications, Minneapolis, 1990), p. 283.
14. *TS Beat* issue 9 (1990), p. 6.